SCIENCE
AND CIVIC LIFE
IN THE
ITALIAN
RENAISSANCE

EUGENIO GARIN is Professor of the History of Philosophy at the University of Florence, where he has both studied and subsequently taught, under various titles, since 1939. A specialist in Renaissance and medieval cultural history, he has had numerous works published in Italian and German.

PETER MUNZ is in the Department of History at the Victoria University of Wellington. In addition to this work he has translated Garin's *Italian Humanism*.

SCIENCE
AND CIVIC LIFE
IN THE
ITALIAN
RENAISSANCE

by
Eugenio Garin

Translated by Peter Munz

ANCHOR BOOKS
Doubleday & Company, Inc.
Garden City, New York

All the essays in this book originally appeared in *Scienza
e vita civile nel Rinascimento italiano,* Editori Laterza,
1965, with the exception of "Interpretations of the Renaissance" and "Magic and Astrology in the Civilisation of the
Renaissance," which originally appeared in *Medioevo e
Rinascimento,* Editori Laterza, 1966.

Anchor Books Edition: 1969

CONTENTS

PREFACE

❡ Most of the present essays originated as lectures. These lectures were given to expound some now well-established results of research. Hence there is a certain lack of critical discussion and documentation. In some cases I have endeavoured to compensate for these defects by giving references to texts in the footnotes and by referring to the researches on which some of my views are based. I am adding this prefatory note in order to clarify my point of view.

My discussion turns upon two points. There is first my interest in the ethical and political ideas and ideals of the Italian cities of the fifteenth century; and secondly there is my interest in the problems of the science of the Renaissance insofar as it was connected with the rebirth of humanistic studies. More generally I hope to show in the present studies how the cultural development, strictly tied in its origins to the life of the Italian city in the fourteenth and fifteenth centuries, came to be one of the preconditions of modern science. However, at the very moment that the new vision of the world was beginning to take shape, the Italian cities and the ideals that had nourished the new image of man began to decline. In the course of two centuries the civilisation of humanism had flourished and the arts had held their triumph. Then there came the metaphysics of Bruno and the science of Galileo. But in the end the cultural hegemony of Italy, which had shown certain signs of national consciousness, declined because of the crisis of civic life in which these forms of humanism had developed. It had all begun with a vigorous political and moral commitment, and it ended with detached contemplation and devotion to the organic growth of autonomous theory.

A great many of the topics here touched upon have been discussed and expounded in a lively fashion both in Italy and abroad.[1] It is widely recognised today that the activities of the humanists were inspired by ethical and political considerations and that the humanists were not just pure grammarians. But there is still some doubt as to whether humanism had any repercussions in philosophy and scientific research. True, nobody today would wish to maintain that science and philosophy developed in *opposition* to the men of letters, that they developed *in spite of* the constant references to ancient texts. But there are quite a few people who, when faced with Valla's and Erasmus' reaction against Aristotle and scholasticism, "express their admiration for the ingenuity of fifteenth-century mathematics and physics and deplore this antipathy, believing the humanists' worship of antiquity to have been harmful to the smooth advance of science."[2] Marie Boas gives expression to an attitude common among historians of science when she emphasises that what the humanists attacked

---

[1] For a different point of view and a well-measured and ample presentation of the problems mentioned see P. O. Kristeller, *Renaissance Thought*, I and II, New York, 1961 and 1965, and the same author's *Eight Philosophers of the Italian Renaissance*, Stanford, California, 1964.

[2] Marie Boas, *The Scientific Renaissance, 1450–1630*, London 1962, pp. 27ff.

in medieval science was not the science but the sterile subtlety of the dialectical discussions *in utramque partem*. For it was precisely this kind of subtlety against which both Leonardo and Galileo were to protest in almost identical terms. Not the least of the humanists' merit in respect to science was their reform of logic. It took the form of a revindication of rhetoric and dialectics in the sphere of the moral sciences and was linked to the recognition of the importance of mathematics for the sciences of nature. On the other hand, Marie Boas continues, "the scientists were prepared to accept the methods of the humanists for a variety of reasons" and above all because in science they found the works of the recent past very inferior to those of the Greek and Roman scientists. For this reason they did not consider it to be against the interest of science to adopt towards Greek texts an attitude very similar to that of the humanists, and often enough they availed themselves of the humanists' mediation—a mediation which was never purely linguistic—in order to find a new approach to ancient scientists. All the same it would be completely erroneous to reduce this development of western civilisation to a collection of libraries of ancient texts offered to the thinkers by "grammarians." The real change was a change in intellectual attitude. "The point was not," A. Koyré wrote,[3] "to combat wrong or insufficient theories but to transform the very frame of intelligence and to turn the old intellectual attitude upside down." There are far too many historians who for the sake of continuity[4] endeavour to present the science of the seventeenth century as the last chapter of medieval knowledge. For this purpose they empty the work of

---

[3] A. Koyré, *Études galiléenes*, I, Paris, 1939, p. 9.
[4] The expression is due to J. Agassi, "Towards a Historiography of Science," *History and Theory*, Suppl. Vol. II, 1963, p. 33.

the fifteenth and sixteenth centuries of all importance because they are unable to accommodate it in the scheme of things past. They are completely unaware of the insidiousness of this alleged continuity which is, in the last analysis, a linear strait-jacket due to scholastic classifications. They prevent themselves from understanding history as a development in which old things decline while new things are not yet fully manifest. New conceptions and the revolutions which bring them about cannot be explained in terms of the past they discard. New perspectives and new methods have to be employed in order to avoid blind alleys and unresolved contradictions. There is much truth in the maxim that in order to jump ahead one has to go back a little.

At the beginning of the fifteenth century the medieval inspiration had reached a point of exhaustion. The Greek inspiration had very much more to offer. But the desire to take up again the scientific inheritance of Greece and the longing for new methods and new horizons did not come from the scientific and philosophical pursuits of the later middle ages. It came from other spheres and it took its cue from ideals that were capable of transforming the image of man and civilisation. The humanistic movement cannot be understood as a linear continuation of the middle ages, for it had its birth in civic life and affected the various fields of knowledge from that angle.

The humanistic culture which flourished in the cities of Italy in the fourteenth and fifteenth centuries manifested itself above all in the field of the moral disciplines by means of a new access to ancient authors. It took concrete shape in new educational methods practised in the schools of grammar and rhetoric. It became a reality in the formation of a new class of administrators of the city-state to whom it offered more refined political techniques. It was used not only in order to compose more efficient official letters but also to formulate programs, to compose treatises and define ideals, to elaborate a conception of life and the meaning of man in society. The words of a past with whose help people intended to establish the continuity of national tradition, the books of authors of whom people proclaimed themselves to be the heirs—all these contributed to the fact that people became more conscious of themselves and began to form a general conception of the history of man.[5] The expositions of the grammarians about the language of ancient texts began to involve all other texts and all other languages, i.e. institutions, habits, norms, procedures in logic and visions of the world. There developed an unprejudiced method of criticism, which took a variety of forms and affected all fields of human activity, making people doubt the very roots

---

[5] This aspect of the activities of the humanists has been at the centre of my researches for thirty years, ever since I first discovered its fruitfulness in a variety of directions. My earliest studies on Salutati's moral thought and the controversy between physicians and lawyers were meant to investigate the roots of these activities. Since then I have changed not only my methods but also my point of view and have reached conclusions somewhat distant from my points of departure. In the course of these researches I have had frequent occasion to use and hold dear some of the early papers by H. Baron, to whom I have always owed a very special debt. I have, however, not been able to use his two major works, *The Crisis of the Early Italian Renaissance* and *Humanistic and Political Literature in Florence and Venice*, both published in 1955. My own *Der italienische Humanismus* (now available in English, as *Italian Humanism*, P. Munz, tr., Oxford, 1966) was first published in 1947. I have also not been able to use some of the studies published outside Italy at the time of the Second World War. I am mentioning these facts only in order to express my regret at the iron laws of chronology, which have prevented me from making full use of certain works by this famous scholar. For the works of Kristeller and Baron and for my own see F. Chabod, *Machiavelli and the Renaissance*, London, 1960, pp. 217–19.

of the authority upon which so much medieval knowledge had been based.

This total change of civilisation was brought about neither under one single heading, nor in a rigid pattern, nor as a straight development. It took place simultaneously in the separate spheres of life. Above all it disturbed the equilibrium of the established outlook. Hence we must conclude that any historiography which seeks to hypostatise and separate the various disciplines that were affected by this disturbance is inadequate because it operates with pseudo-categories. It sees the pursuit of letters on one side and science and philosophy on the other. If one accepts this historiography one loses all sense of how the different aspects of human activity belong together and will overlook the fact that the fundamental attitudes and synthetic visions which govern the progress of civilisation have their centre of gravity in a dominant form which eventually informs every single manifestation.[6] The various activities and disciplines never remain substantially the same, and therefore the relationships between these disciplines keep changing. In a society in which the predominant experience is a religious one, all general ideas will tend to appear under the sign of religion. And in a society in which artistic and scientific activities begin to predominate, the whole centre of gravity of civilised life is bound to be changed. In 1961 A. Koyré in his *La révolution astronomique* (i.e. the history of a revolution in knowledge under the sign of astronomy) wrote that "the mind's pilgrimage towards truth never follows a straight line: it is necessary to follow it along all its tortuous paths."

Between the beginning of the fourteenth century

---

[6] E. A. Burt, in his important *The Metaphysical Foundations of Modern Physical Science*, London, 1925, stressed the links between the history of science, its revolutions, and the history of metaphysics.

and the end of the fifteenth, society's equilibrium was disturbed. Humanists, artists, artisans, and men of action replaced old medieval habits by a new impetus, new ideas, and a new ferment. Investigations which had so far remained without results were suddenly diverted into fruitful channels. In a complex and disconcerting crisis new ideas and new theories were evolved. An old way of seeing reality disappeared and a new way emerged. Magic and science, poetry and philosophy were suddenly brought into contact with each other in a society that was being troubled by religious doubts as well as by all manner of practical requirements. The new ideas fertilised each other and made nonsense of all rigid schemes of thought.

But if one insists upon looking at these centuries from the vantage points of St. Thomas or Duns Scotus (or, for that matter, from the vantage point of Descartes and Spinoza), Pico and Ficino, Pomponazzi and Telesio will hardly stand out and Valla and Poliziano will appear as mere pedants. Even Leonardo and Galileo, viewed as only the tail end of certain medieval developments, will be reduced to mere objects of curiosity.

There have been historians who have tried to identify humanism as a mere movement of pre-Tridentine catholic apologetics. In the eyes of these historians the whole of the civilisation of the Renaissance was no more than a scholastic movement which took place in academic rhetoric and philosophy. Thus they arrive at a rigid opposition between humanistic literature and philosophy (or science) understood as a re-reading of classical authors such as Plato, Aristotle, Galen, Euclid, and Archimedes. They see this opposition as a parallel to the opposition between orthodox rhetoric and heretical Graeco-Arabic science. The whole of the Renaissance according to this view was no more than a modest chapter written by thinkers of very mediocre speculative talent, and is dwarfed by the great theological synthesis of the middle ages on one side and the grand philosophico-scientific systems of the seventeenth century on the other. With admirable erudition the upholders of this view have accumulated more and more materials and unknown texts in order to show up the would-be dreamers of new worlds, the unquiet spirits and rebels against tradition that the thinkers of the Renaissance had imagined themselves to be, as inane rhetoricians and commentators. What had been thought of as an age of crisis, of mental revolution and fruitful illumination, thus became an age of pedants and scholars. The breach with the past was obscured and so was the birth of new types of intellect, of a new circulation of ideas in schools as well as in courts and cities, in shops and banks, among magistrates, politicians, and men of action, i.e. among laymen in a lay society. The intellectual and spiritual repercussions of discoveries such as those of Columbus and Copernicus were forgotten, and the whole air of radical renewal which had informed scientists as well as philosophers and had made them agree that one had to begin again at the beginning, was ignored.

Some of the essays collected in this volume deal with the practical, ethical, and political aspects of the renewal of culture which took place in the fourteenth and fifteenth centuries under the sign of a return to the classics. Literary production and political writings were closely intertwined, and it is impossible to separate the humanists' literary and private work from their official and public activities. This fact demonstrates how certain forms of expression came to be welded to political requirements and how closely the fate of rhetoric and of the new conception of life depended on the emergence and the eventual decline of a certain society.

The study of the ancient authors was always linked to actual and contemporary experience: the one fertilised the other. Hence it is impossible to understand the great personalities of the period without understanding their public activities and hence it is necessary to connect the rhetoric of the humanists and their preoccupation with ancient writers with political life. All this emerges as something very different from a mere chapter in the history of the schools of grammar.

It is obvious that a serious attempt to understand men like Salutati, Bruni, and Acciaiuoli can derive much profit from a more detailed research into the social status and the property of the humanists.[7] One will thereby obtain a more lively and a more complete picture. But it cannot change the meaning of the program of the humanists, of their battles and their standpoints. Above all it cannot affect the connection between their literary studies, their studies of ancient history, and the realities of contemporary politics. I dwell particularly on these connections to prevent a reduction of the rhetoric and grammar of the humanists to a mere event in the history of the schools or literature.

On the other hand if one calls attention to the connection between culture and practical activity one can follow the whole development of the civilisation of the Renaissance and distinguish its phases. The obvious change of ideas and ideals, of books and authors, which made the Florence of Salutati so different from the Florence of Ficino and which had its repercussions in art as well as in poetry, in philosophy

---

[7] For a contribution on this matter cp. L. Martines, *The Social World of Florentine Humanists*, Princeton, 1963. It is interesting to recall a remark by Antonio Labriola in a letter to F. Engels of August 3, 1894, on the connection between Chancellor Salutati, "the first humanist . . . the true bourgeoisie . . . which begins to dominate Florence," and the economic theories of St. Bernardino and St. Antonino. "The Italy of that day," he concluded, "is the prehistory of capitalism."

as well as in rhetoric, has to be traced back to political history. Even if I do not dwell on causes it is useful for the historical understanding of culture to underline both obvious connections and hidden relations and to investigate the groups who propagated the various ideas and defended them. In this way one can substitute a consideration of specific events for a consideration of general terms. To give a single example: the decline of the hegemony of the humanistic culture of a Bruni and a Salutati and the emergence of that theology so dear to Ficino and his followers will appear to be something very different from the personal conversion of a few scholars from the pursuit of letters to philosophy. It will not be possible to reduce the tremendous change to an internal event in the pious soul of an individual intent upon affirming the continuity of the Platonic tradition in the middle ages.

The following pages are meant to call attention to still another point. They are meant to remind us that we can make a contribution to an understanding of the development of science by focussing our attention not upon abstract questions, but upon close investigations of minute problems, that is upon definite men and definite groups. It has been customary when investigating the scientific and philosophical interests of the humanists to think of heterogeneity and to stress the differences between the different periods. This habit has led to a denial of the fact that there was a free circulation of ideas among artists, scholars, and artisans. Investigators have thus obscured the connection between the renewal of the sciences and the elaboration of general ideas by men of letters and philosophers, and have forgotten that a great many fruitful hypotheses were first formulated by mystical and magical thinking. Similarly they have tended to overlook the fact that many technological inventions owed their efficacy to the cultural transformation. And equally have historians passed over in silence the fact that the evolution of rhetoric had a great effect on the development of both mathematics and the logic of the sciences of nature. History has too often been written in terms of black and white, in terms of grand categories. Historians have seen on one side an elusive Platonism, and on the other a rigorous Aristotelianism; on one side, Ficino's mysticism, and on the other, the uneducated Leonardo; on one side the Neoplatonic and Hermetic philosophers, and on the other, Galileo with his telescope and the arsenal of Venice. But the truth is that Copernicus availed himself of Platonic concepts for his masterpiece; that Galileo did not battle against Platonism, but against Peripateticism; that men like Leonardo found delight in writings about the sun which disconcertingly breathed the air of Ficino's style; that William Harvey prefaced his *magnum opus* with a text that we could just as easily have found in Pico. Although some people tend to belittle these observations by attributing them to a passing fashion, they remain of fundamental importance. The heart of the matter is that we must today be mindful of these facts because they loomed so large in the minds of the men of the period we are writing about.

The documents indeed tell a different story. Recently the attempt has been made to reconstruct one of the most significant chapters in the history of medieval science (and of philosophy), that concerning the problem of perspective and its implications for the anatomy of actual vision as well as for the field of astronomy and astrology. The point of departure for this attempt is a Codex of great importance which used to be in the Library of San Marco in Florence and which, as far as some of its contents are concerned, is unique. The Codex in question is an organic collection of fundamental texts by Oresmus, Henry of Langenstein, Domenico da Chivasso, and others, put together approximately in 1400. But the most important fact is that this MS forms part

of a body of very valuable scientific writings collected by Ser Filippo di Ser Ugolino Pieruzzi da
Vertine, who became *Notaro delle Riformagioni* in
1429 but whose activities can be traced back to 1401.
He was a humanist—and according to the classifications so dear to certain historians, because of his opposition to the Medici he should have been destined,
after 1444, to end up as a teacher of Latin in a minor
country school. But if one peruses the MSS of Ser
Filippo which are today preserved in the *Biblioteca
Laurenziana* and the *Biblioteca Nazionale* of Florence
one gains the very clear impression that one is confronting a magnificent library of ancient and medieval
science, collected with rare competence by a great
scholar who was interested in mathematics, physics,
astronomy, and astrology. I do not intend to analyse
these books. This was done at the beginning of the
century by A. A. Björnbo in a series of contributions
which deserve great attention, for they brought to
light a unique document of scientific interest written
between the end of the fourteenth century and the
first decades of the fifteenth century in Florence, that
high seat of humanistic studies. The evidence as to
who owned some of these writings is no less illuminating. The *Perspectiva* of John Peckam (ms. *Conv.
Sopp.*I.v.25), for instance, appears to have passed
from the hands of Salutati through those of Ser
Filippo to Niccoli and to Cosimo the Elder. It was
finally published by Fazio Cardano and used and
quoted by Leonardo da Vinci.[8]

The question of the treatises on perspective would

---

[8] The descriptions by A. A. Björnbo were published as a
series of articles from 1903 onwards in the third series of the
Bibliotheca Mathematica under the title "Die mathematischen
S. Marcohandschriften in Florenz." The ms. referred to, Naz.
Firenze, *Conv. Sopp.* J.x.19, is the point of departure of G.
Federici Vescovini, *Studi sulla prospettiva medievale,* Torino,
1965.

carry us far. But we might at least remind ourselves
of the ms. *Conv.*J.v.30, one of the Codices of Ser
Filippo. It was recently brought to our attention by
Marshall Clagett because of its importance for what
he has called "the Florence versions" of Archimedes'
De Mensura Circuli.[9] As far as we can make out from

---

[9] M. Clagett, *Archimedes in the Middle Ages*, Vol. I, *The
Arabo-Latin Tradition*, Madison, Wisconsin, 1964, pp. 91–142.
The precious material collected by Clagett is, among other
things, also important because it shows how modest Archimedes' role was in the middle ages. See esp. p. 14. A. Koyré,
op. cit., I, p. 10, n. 1, observed as follows: "I think that one
could sum up the scientific work of the sixteenth century as a
gradual reception and understanding of Archimedes. As far as
the history of science is concerned the popular conception of
the Renaissance is profoundly true."

For a lively and exact determination of the importance of
Archimedes and the Greek mathematicians see N. W. Gilbert,
"Galileo and the School of Padua," *Journal of the History of
Philosophy*, I, 1963, pp. 223–31. Gilbert objects to the theories
of J. H. Randall, Jr., *The School of Padua and the Emergence
of Modern Science*, Padua, 1961. Gilbert denies that Galileo
derived his own method from the Aristotelian logicians of
Padua. He thinks that Galileo based himself on Euclid, Archimedes, and Pappo. He insists, rightly, that the renewed discussions on method stemmed from the rereading of the Platonic dialogues. In this connection I would like to refer to
what I wrote with reference to the debate with Randall in my
"Gli umanisti e la scienza" *Rivista di filosofia*, Vol. 52, 1961,
pp. 259–78. There is one point, however, p. 227, where Gilbert,
though right in substance, is not wholly exact. It is not true
that there are no considerations of logic in Galileo's *Juvenilia*.
As I will mention later, Favaro omitted the notes for
Dialectica. Randall also took no notice of them. These notes,
however, even if they do not refer to the Peripatetic logicians
of Padua by name, are full of the echoes of these men. But
this does not detract from Gilbert's observations.

Too often one makes the mistake of thinking that the
influence of the new logic or of the new rhetoric on the
formation of the new science was direct, i.e. that the natural
philosophers took over the techniques of the rhetoricians and

the *Life* of Ser Filippo by Vespasiano, Ser Filippo was personally acquainted with Bruni, Traversari, Manetti, and Marsuppini. He knew Greek and was in touch with all the scholarly circles of the city. Thus we come to Toscanelli, to his knowledge of mathematics and his discussions with Cusanus, his researches into perspective, both natural and artificial, and to his scientific relations with Brunelleschi.[10] If we survey this road we will also find not only the treatises collected by Ghiberti (whose *Commentarii*, it seems, were begun in 1448) but also the more complex activities of Alberti. All this amounted to a unique encounter between the most refined humanistic culture, art, and science. One could consider Alberti a symbol which gives the lie to the belief that there was an opposition between literature and science, between humanism and naturalism, between the world of the artists and the world of the scholars. Through the mouth of his Momo, Alberti gave us a eulogy of the divinely rational nature which regulates everything and eternally animates all things living. As is well known, Alberti believed that laws and rational principle were present in reality. He fought and ridiculed magical and astrological superstitions. In another work he tells us of a very scholarly astronomer and famous scientist of Bologna. When this worthy man became a father he cast his son's horoscope and discovered that his son would be hanged. In order to

---

the dialecticians. The truth is that they availed themselves of them indirectly. They either treasured their criticism or took notice of the fact that as derived from Aristotle these techniques ought to remain confined more properly to morals and politics.

[10] Cp. A. Parronchi, *Studi su la "dolce" prospettiva*, Rome, 1964. Among others, Parronchi published the small treatise *Della prospettiva*. A. Bonucci attributed it to Alberti, but Parronchi, p. 581–641, attributes it to Toscanelli.

avoid this fate he made him become a religious, because priests could not be hanged. In spite of everything, and in spite of the fact that the son was a veritable model of virtue and thus seemed to remain immune to destiny and fate, when the hour indicated by the stars approached, the good father persuaded his son to have himself hanged fictitiously in front of some friends and with a certain amount of emotion, so that the stars could have their due and their influence be exorcised. The young man, unaware of the intention, had lent himself to these proceedings out of filial piety. He was apprised of the trick during the euphoria which followed the danger he had escaped, turned bitterly against the scientific inanity of astrology and against the moral teachings he had treasured and inveighed against the belief that the wise man is master of the stars. Soon after, at the appointed hour, there was a riot in the city and several ruffians, who feared the young man's well-known respect for the law, hanged him.

One is tempted to discuss other writings by Alberti about his theories on *Fortuna* and *virtù*. They are informed by a critical mind and a lack of dogmatism. He was aware of the importance of human effort but also found that, mysteriously, all human effort had its limits. Alberti was both scientist and artist, a man of letters and a philosopher, and when one is reading Erasmus and Bruno, Leonardo da Vinci and Ariosto, one cannot help but remember him. He was echoed by the greatest thinkers and scientists as well as the greatest poets and writers, in the *Sogno di Polifilo* as well as in the *Orlando furioso*.

The present essays deal with the world of this culture and seek to determine some of its most significant components.

E. G.

Florence
April 1965

SCIENCE
AND CIVIC LIFE
IN THE
ITALIAN
RENAISSANCE

INTERPRETATIONS
OF THE RENAISSANCE

❡ There is today a lively interest in the problem of
the Renaissance which impells many people to take
another look at Renaissance Humanism. This new
interest is not entirely due, it seems to me, to the fact
that after so many attempts all purely historical interpretations of the Renaissance have been exhausted.
There was a time when many of us were seduced by
these historical interpretations. But now there is not a
single such interpretation which satisfies our method-
ological demands. Too many new problems have come
to our knowledge. They define and help us to understand a great many aspects and motifs which used to
be either neglected or obscured by the purely historical approach. There can be little doubt that any
purely historical interpretation of the Renaissance
creates more problems than it solves. But in the last
instance, the crisis through which all purely historical
interpretations of the Renaissance are going results
from our need to give an account of the essential and
directive lines of thought in western civilisation. This
need continuously turns us back upon what is, after all,
a crucial period in the history of the west. The
Renaissance was indeed a crucial period—not only in
the history of philosophy in the narrow sense in

which philosophy is a discipline concerned with the technical discussion of certain defined problems, but in the history of the view of the life of man. For it was precisely during this time that the horizons of the most serious of all researches began to alter. As a result there disappeared, even though many people were not fully aware of it at the time, a well-established and venerable form of philosophising. The truth is that at this time there emerged, once and for all, a new manner of seeing the world, and an ancient way of seeing it disappeared. True, the old manner of seeing it disappeared in a blaze of glory, for the old manner had aspects which gave rise to the new manner. But all in all it did amount to a solemn burial of a dead, if noble, interpretation of reality. The only thing is that that burial was not accomplished all at once. The knowledge that the old world was dying matured very slowly and agonisingly. And it is perhaps only today that we can fully understand the catastrophic conclusion of this process. The centre of interest was shifted from one method of research to another. A complete change in the relationships between man and the ultimate realities, between man and things, between man and human institutions took place. And all this bore witness to a total change in man's attitude. If one goes to the bottom of things, these changes indicate the end of a sense of security and the beginning of an age of torment. The direction the new search was to take was at first not clear, for the new conception of the "free" man was placed in the very margin of the destruction of all preconceived forms: "you, who are neither a citizen of heaven nor a citizen of the earth, neither mortal nor immortal, you are, by yourself almost free and a sovereign creator. You must shape and hew yourself in an image which you must choose for yourself."

There was a way of writing history which pictured this rebirth of the free man as something like a triumphal march of certainties and resounding achievements. But if one peruses the most important testimonies of that age, and I am thinking chiefly of the fifteenth century, one will all the time discover that people, instead of being conscious of a beginning, were dimly aware that something was ending. The ending they sensed, though glorious, was nevertheless an ending. True, there is no lack of reminders that something new was being constructed. And there were assurances that man is indeed capable of carrying out a reconstruction of the world and of himself. But there was also an awareness of the fact that the secure tranquillity of a homely and familiar universe, ordered and adjusted to our needs, was lost forever. Even where the most ancient themes lingered on, they changed in tone and flavour. Thus people kept believing that perhaps our illnesses are written in the stars. But in such cases they ceased to think of astral communications as the work of benevolent celestial deities and interpreted them as signs of man's sad enslavement to obscure and indifferent forces, beyond man's grasp. For this reason, people came to think of the liberation from astral destiny as a liberation from man's annihilation by things. To free man from the tyranny of the stars meant to free him from the anxiety of not being able to achieve anything or be anything.

Today we derive great pleasure from reading those new praises of nature and hymns to the infinite. But this is only because we somehow imagine that there was a tranquil confidence which kept shining through; or at least because we keep having a confident hope that the infinite which was promised was something positive. The sense of loss which ran through the whole of that civilisation thereby escapes us. For that civilisation, once it had smashed the ancient idols, was aware of the boundary it had reached, and knew of its own responsibility before unknown possibilities. A fine example of this is the spiritual itinerary of Ficino, who had come to the infinity of nature through Lucretius.

In that infinite nature, man, because of his substance, has no prerogatives. Later he discovered that same loss and that same indifference to the meaning life once was supposed to have had in the immobile and timeless rigidity of the thought of Averroës and in the Aristotelianism of Alexander of Aphrodisia. It was then that he donned the garments of a priest and turned towards Plato and Plotinus in order to find someone who might transform into hope the restlessness that troubled him, and to assure him that the meaning which we are unable to discover here on earth, the positive certainty of things, is in reality up on high, where it will be revealed to us in the end. Both his Christianity and his Platonism helped him to keep alive at least one comforting doubt: "perhaps things as they appear to us are not true; perhaps, at present, we are asleep." Hence emerged the Ficino who was more sincere and more lively than the one who arranged everything in well-ordered and systematic concepts and substances which he could then place as a screen between himself and his bewilderment. His systematic universe was as fictitious as it was comforting. It was solidified in a reassuring hierarchy in which even the much celebrated dignity of man tended to vanish, for there was always the risk that the idea that man stood in the centre would reduce itself to the mere determination of a spatial locality.

There was another sense and another courage in the rich appeal to human virtue, to a virtue capable of overcoming destiny, capable of changing that destiny and constructing its own world and of giving a new shape to things with the help of that human artfulness which joins science and poetry. This, indeed, was the meaning of the civic humanism of Florence in the fifteenth century. This meaning inspired both Albert and Pico when they transformed rhetorical and philological humanism into the metaphysics of man the creator. This metaphysics, I believe, was the most profound part of the whole of the Renaissance.

If we regard the ideas of Alberti as typical it would be wrong to see in his idea of virtue nothing more than the joyful certainty of a man confident of his actions and unaware that he is standing on the edge of an abyss. Just because Alberti is always a poet, and that means a creator, he was well aware of the risk involved in all creativity, in every construction which amounts to bringing about a fundamental change in what is given to us and indeed in the whole world. He was very aware of how unstable all constructions are and how in the very end all virtue will be vanquished. Campano wrote that there is no man whose virtue is not defeated in one last battle, be it only the one with death, for all human beings and all things are destined to perish.

One ought to remember that Alberti's sadness was not a well-articulated pessimism. It was simply nourished by the knowledge that everything must change. Alberti had experienced many economic and political changes in his own home and had watched a whole mode of life disappear before his eyes. All this made him extremely thoughtful about the insecurity of life. His beautiful dialogue *Fatum et Fortuna* is one of the most deeply serious works in our whole moral literature; it eliminates all chances of optimism. The man who wants to know too much is aware of the shadows that darken the tempestuous river of life, and they remind him how vain it is for beings who are allowed to know only through sense experience to seek to understand God. And just as there is a limit to knowledge, there is also a limit to action. One cannot escape the rapids and falls of the river *Bios*. They form stumbling-blocks and ambushes which will sooner or later break every ship, even when a calm and free mind, with the help of the arts, can maintain it within certain limits and guide its course safely for a certain distance. The ultimate truth is harsh: "I have understood that fate determines the course of everything in the life of man and that it runs its course according to its law . . . I have also understood that for us, *Fortuna* is hard, if we have to be drowned in the river at the very moment when we ought to be fighting the violence of the wave with a strong arm: nevertheless we cannot ignore that in human affairs prudence and industry count for much."

These reservations insistently recall the obscurity of the foundations of life and its uncertainties. They are a reminder of the ineluctable limits set on all our efforts to determine our fate. Everything in this vision reminds one of the myth of Er in which the element of fortuity that is present at the launching of every fate is emphasised by the blindness that is at the very root of the human condition. The wise builder, the master of architecture was to tell us, constructs solid buildings, capable of withstanding the ravages of time. The many calculations by which he has dealt with even the most minute natural forces are hidden. For the artist's dreams are not dreamt in a state of intoxication. On the contrary, the artist builds on the basis of a detailed and prudent plan; and he builds things that will be fruitful and useful. He will always bear in mind his own interests and those of his friends. But in spite of everything, the edifice must one day fall to pieces. There can be no such thing as absolute stability. Everything decays: even the things that have taken their inspiration from absolute stability, stable goodness and stable truth, including those things which pretend to have been built according to absolute rules. And when they decay, they do not decay because of the malignity of men or because of the adversity of matter. They decay because in our world there is no such thing as a fixed rule and an absolute certainty. "There was a time . . . when I was in the habit of basing my views on truth, my zeal on considerations of utility, my words and expressions on my innermost thoughts. . . . But I have learnt now to adapt my views to the prevailing superstitions, my zeal to caprices, and to frame all my words so as to be capable of deception." These myths console us and create the illusions and seductions of our daily life. They are like the many branches of the ivy into which Momo transformed himself so as to be able to embrace, possess, and corrupt the beautiful daughter of virtue.

One could say that Alberti's mood was no more than a pleasantry, a bitter way of telling a tale, an expression of contempt, perhaps a joke. But the very opposite is true. The full flavour of his *Momus* comes out in the way that gaiety is made to appear serious. The *Momus* is meant to demonstrate the validity of a caprice, the philosophy of a mere poet, the non-philosophy of the philosopher. In reality, the philosopher himself is an extraordinary myth-maker. He calls these myths "systems." As Telesio was to observe in all seriousness, these systems fashion whole worlds according to his arbitrary will in competition with God. The worst aspect of these philosophical constructions is that they are so often ugly, inconsistent, sterile, and serious to the point of boredom whereas the artist has at his disposal the imagination of very life itself, and he builds even as life builds and makes no claims for his creations over and above their own inherent value. The world of the artist is the world of living imagination just as the world of nature is the living imagination of God. The artist is a creator and his forms take shape, rejoice and appear among us, live with us and transform our lives as the fables of ancient superstition were wont to do. In the *Momus*, Charon says something which is on the face of it quite trivial but he gives it immediately a new subtle interpretation: "you, who know the course of the stars but are ignorant of human affairs, you are indeed a fine philosopher! I will not report the opinions of a philosopher—for all your science, you philosophers, is limited to verbal subtleties. I will relate instead what I have heard from a painter. That painter, when he observes the shapes of bodies, sees more things than all you philosophers together have ever seen in your efforts to measure and explore the skies." Charon then shows us what it is that the painter has seen when he prefers the loving observation of flowers to rational and speculative discourse. When he hears of subtle doctrines, he is stupefied and demands to know why "you neglect flowers when in a single flower all things combine into beauty and gracefulness . . ." Alberti's main theme is life in its spontaneity. He talks about the function of artists and poets as it was to be understood later by Vico. Hence he finds nourishment for his disconcerting praise of the vagabond, of the man who breaks all bonds and restraints and who refuses to accept any position as absolute; of the man who is free and who is, in spite of his gay caprices, fundamentally serious—for he is aware of the non-value of all sacred values as well as of the value of what seems mere folly. Alberti's *Momus* is much less famous than Erasmus' *Praise of Folly*. But often enough it touches upon very profound matters. In the end, it furnishes a lavish proclamation of the importance of myth. It includes a critique of religious myths and recognises the validity of myth-making for the life of man. But in spite of all this not one of the venerable forms of the most authoritative traditions is salvaged—neither philosophy (except perhaps Socratic irony) nor religion, which is finally demolished by Charon: "If I were by myself I would just laugh at it. But among so many people I pretend to respect it." If Momus had continued his tales, the gods would have been dispersed in next to no time. For this reason Alberti silenced him by a curious final reminder of the limit—a reminder which recalls his *Fatum et Fortuna*. Hence, Alberti's "dispersal," contained in this kind of irony and therefore essentially ambiguous, is very different from the enthusiastic and confident "dispersal" of Bruno. Bruno's "dispersal" came close to blasphemy but ended up by re-assembling in its own way all the gods, all the laws, and all the old certainties—amounting, therefore, perhaps to no more than the rebellion of a penitent. Alberti's dispersal, in spite of its vague tone, is a very terrible one in that it reminds man of the full responsibility with which it is fraught. For after the dispersal the consoling and well-systematised world of the metaphysicians, as well as the no less tranquil and reassuring world of the gods, is gone forever. Even if an infinitely far-away and unknowable absolute God were to be invoked or rejected, man's situation in the universe could never be changed again. Lefèvre d' Étaples was to give us a description of Pico della Mirandola. When he was carried away by the most powerful wave of Savonarolan faith, Pico intoned a moving prayer in the Lucretian manner and bemoaned the fact that God was so far-away.

Bruno was solidly confident that he would be able to open a passage through the shattered walls of the world and that that passage would lead towards the all embracing One, the absolute which was well worth one's infinite love and the truth of which was a guarantee of the positive sense of reality. Bruno, and Cusanus before him, supply good arguments against those who reason that the culture of the Renaissance was a continuation of traditional culture. Both thinkers were men who had undertaken the construction of a metaphysical system and had thus taken up the traditional themes inherent in the logic of every speculation. They had not succeeded in determining the structure of reality by fixing necessary and stable forms. A truly "humanistic" standpoint, rather, has to be a poetical one. It proceeds by ignoring scholastic philosophy, or at least by considering it as something foreign. It has to remain deaf to it. A humanistic approach has to refute scholasticism as something which exhausts itself in the elaboration of rational schemes and paradigms that not only fail to explain or unravel reality but also have absolutely nothing to do with it. It is for this reason that Alberti never speaks of the actual infinity of man or of his substantial dignity, either of which might serve to reassure man about his transcendental destiny. He always speaks instead of the infinite number of human possibilities which, in the manner of a good humanist, he emphasises. These possibilities are the many mundane possibilities of the architect, the poet, the builder and the administrator of the city, the merchant and the householder. In the last analysis we are to be consoled in our melancholy position by beautiful fables and myths. Every time we approach the Renaissance we sense that its truth is to be found in Valla, Alberti, and Poliziano, in its Masaccios, Brunelleschis, Leonardos, Michelangelos, and Galileos —that is, in the artists, poets, historians and philologists, scientists—and last but not least in politicians and historians like Guicciardini and Machiavelli as well as in a prophet and reformer like Savonarola. It is not that this period is without its philosophers and could not have made its contribution to philosophy or that if it did, it only impinged upon the most obstruse parts of metaphysics, ontology, and gnoseology. It is rather that the most conscious form of human speculation took place in the sphere of philology, history, and science, all of which were opposed to the traditional ways of philosophising, which were busy "competing with God" instead of seeking to understand the world in order to change it and subject it to human requirements. This was the manner in which Telesio, for one, defined the difference between the old and the new way. It was no accident that the historico-philological attitudes, in the widest meaning of the term, proved a critical consummation and consolidation of the ancient way of viewing the world. While the old Aristotelian physics, in one last and fatal crisis, was dying of exhaustion, there emerged into full daylight a body of magical and alchemical doctrines consisting of techniques which could change the world. And in their wake came the irreverent experimental arts designed to break all laws and subvert all order. They were destined to move the stars from their courses, to transform all living beings, and to bring the dead to life. Men like Francis Bacon, Giordano Bruno, and Tommaso Campanella were to be among those who were seduced by the fascination of the experimental arts. It is worth recalling that in this environment there was nourished the theory that truth is the daughter of time; for, as magicians and astrologers were only too quick to notice, the certainties of today can only be slowly built by conquering the errors of the past. This was not likely to be done by people who seek to deduce once and for all the rational order of the world *a priori* but only by people who are engaged in the laborious pursuit of experimentation.

Towards the end of the fifteenth century, in a work which could well be compared with the *Discourse on Method* and the *Novum Organum*, Giovanni Pico della Mirandola defined the implications of the new image of man with great precision. He considered that the essence of the new image was man's independence of every predetermined species of form, as if man were breaking the bounds of the world of forms, as if he were the lord not only of his own form but also, through magic, the lord of the whole world of forms which he might combine with one another, transform, or remake. At the same time, reinterpreting the very ancient doctrine that the universe was a grand book of great originality, he demonstrated how historico-philological research coincided with the investigation of nature and how the world of man coincided with the world of nature provided the latter was transfigured and humanised by the effort of man. On the other hand he tended to intrude a religious element into this vision of man. He managed to achieve this through his historical critique of astrology as an astral religion and through his attempt to explain the biblical narratives by precise methods. In this way humanism attempted to become aware of its own radically new implications. It laid down the precise limits of the validity of a philosophy which, in Italy, was to continue along the royal road of historico-philological research. On this road we find Galileo, Vico, Muratori, to mention only the greatest names. This refutes Spaventi's theory that after the Renaissance philosophy emigrated from Italy. The theory, with all due respect to the subtle philosopher that Spaventi was, was due to a failure to understand fully the meaning and the inheritance of the humanistic ideal of the Renaissance.

We are bound to misunderstand the genuine significance of the Renaissance if we do not appreciate the proper meaning of humanism and keep on seeking its secret in the writings of a belated grammarian or in an alleged continuity with the middle ages. At the same time, the humanistic praise of the dignity of man can easily lead to a facile rhetoric if one does not bear in mind the price which had to be paid for it. The price was indeed high: one had to pay for the freedom to fight in a world that was stubbornly opposed to any effort and in which progress was difficult by relinquishing the reassuring idea that a given order existed. One also had to abandon the belief in a justice which would always in the end, albeit sometimes by very obscure means, triumph. What emerged instead was a political life without illusions, in which people were buffeted by forces without pity and in which the vanquished were eliminated without compassion. Similarly, people began to sense that everything in the world was frail and that God, if a God remained, was terribly faraway and ineffable and likely to issue unintelligible decrees to punish the just and save the sinner—a God to Whom it was vain to address prayers. If it is necessary to mention names, one need only think of

Machiavelli and Pomponazzi, of Luther and Calvin as well as of the faces sculpted by Michelangelo. And finally, with Copernicus, Bruno, and Galileo, there came the end of the homely and well-ordered Ptolemaic system.

Once this is understood, one can give proper emphasis to the question of what precisely was new in the thought of the Renaissance. From a number of different standpoints attempts have been made to push back the Renaissance to the twelfth century or even to the Carolingian age and even to deny that apart from literary and artistic development, there ever emerged anything that was really new. It would be no exaggeration to say that much of modern historical writing about the origin of modern thought is devoted to the attempt to demolish the conventional view that there was anything like a break between one way of thinking about the universe and another way. Admittedly this reaction was encouraged by the fact that the upholders of this view used to take their stand on arguments which are only too easily discounted. It is perfectly true that such things as a love for pagan antiquity and the classical writers, a lack of piety or of religion, atheism, naturalism, and radical immanentism can without difficulty be traced back into the middle ages. In this sense it has actually been helpful to stress and illustrate the continuity between the middle ages and the world of humanism and, for that matter, between the ancient world and the middle ages. In this way it has been possible to document the fact that humanism did not amount to a rebirth of ancient culture because ancient culture had always been alive throughout the middle ages, at least since the twelfth century. This view, when all is said and done, was not even very new, for it had been a not infrequent habit among the writers of the fifteenth and sixteenth centuries to trace the Renaissance back to Dante, a position that was propounded with some

solemnity in the *Commentari urbani* of Raffaele da
Volterra. Similarly, the argument that the Renaissance
goes back to the days of Charlemagne and Alcuin
was not invented by modern French medievalists; it
was put forward by Filippo de' Medici, Archbishop of
Pisa and Florentine ambassador to Paris on the occasion of the coronation of Louis XI. He mentioned it in
his official speech in 1461 and referred to an explicit
statement in the Letter Dedicatory to the Sovereign of
the *Vita di Carlo Magno,* presented as a formal gift
by Donato Acciaiuoli.

However this may be, it is certainly one of the
merits of modern historical research to have understood that the myth of rebirth, of the new light, and
hence the corresponding conception of a preceding
darkness was the result of the attacks made by the
humanists themselves upon the culture of the preceding centuries. There can be no doubt that the writers
of the fifteenth century insisted with exasperating
repetitiveness of the fact that they had revolted
against an age of barbarism in order to bring about an
age of humaneness (*humanitas*). It is equally beyond
doubt that in the preceding centuries the sense of
rapid historical development had never been as lively.
From every corner emerged the idea that an old world
was on the wane, and wherever people looked they
found confirmation of the view that an established
vision of the world was being abandoned. The new
discoveries broke the traditional image of the world,
and the old conception of the universe was shaken
long before Galileo. Ever since criticism had destroyed the psychological premisses of the Ptolemaic
system, it had become necessary to face the consequences of the idea that the universe was infinite,
that there were other inhabited worlds and that the
earth was not in a privileged position. There is no
need to enlarge upon the effects that ideas and observations of this kind had on theology. The curious
thing is that modern historiography, in its attempt to

grasp the idea the Renaissance had of itself, has managed to stand this idea on its head by denying that it included any element of newness. If it is true that the light-darkness opposition is very old and goes back to an ancient religious tradition, and if it is therefore true that the alleged contrast between the darkness of the middle ages and the consequent rebirth was nothing more than an occasion for a conventional controversy, then all insistence upon a break and the emergence of something new is of doubtful value. As a result of much critical work it has now been clearly established that much of what we believed to belong to the Renaissance goes back to the middle ages. People in the middle ages loved the classics no less than people in the Renaissance. Everybody knew their Aristotle in the middle ages—and perhaps they knew him better than the people of the fifteenth century. Even Plato was known in the middle ages and by no means only indirectly. Ancient poets, historians, and orators were known and appreciated. Bernardo Silvestre had written philosophical poems worthy of Bruno; Bernard of Chartres had been aware that truth was the daughter of time, and jurists had been busy reconstructing the whole essence of Roman wisdom. The revaluation of man had been more powerfully and profoundly conceived by St. Thomas than by Ficino. Furthermore, the naturalism and lack of piety of Machiavelli, Pomponazzi, and Bruno, even where they seemed most bold and most new, turned out to be quite old. In fact, these men were the heirs, more or less consciously so, of medieval Alexandrism (condemned as early as 1210) and of Averroism and, through Arabic science, of other Hellenistic currents.

In this way the recognition that both in content and in problems there was nothing very original in the Renaissance as far as the history of thought was concerned forced some people to regard humanism as an aspect of *studia humanitatis* understood in a narrow sense as grammatical studies. They alleged that such studies assumed in the fourteenth century a major importance. But not even here did these people allow that something really new had happened. At most, they assigned to the rhetorical arts a somewhat more dignified place than they had occupied before. One is tempted to say that with this conclusion the academic controversy resounded in favour of the grammarians. Grammarians, it was held, had simply continued their customary labours which they had never interrupted; but now they were translating more accurately and more widely—though even this is doubted by some. Thus they were said to have diffused a more solid knowledge of both Latin and Greek, but indirectly, with a consequence which was always purely marginal. It is curious that this argument completely obscured the importance of the Salutati, the Bruni, the Poggio, of men who had been the great exponents of the highest culture and of a grand epoch, of citizens, magistrates, thinkers, and all this in order to vindicate in a facile manner the continuity of the scholastic habits of a whole lot of second-rate compilers of knowledge. Looked at from this angle, even Valla's philology, instead of bearing the imprint of an era of rebellion, is reduced to a burnt-out case.

It was quite justifiable to make an attempt to understand the slow process by which a grand period of culture had blossomed and matured. But in the end this attempt misfired so completely that the preoccupation with minute forms crowded out all sense of proportion. The same error which had been at the basis of the old interpretations had proved fatal in this case. The old interpretations sought to discover what exactly was new in the Renaissance by comparison with the middle ages. It might have been useful to observe that there was a correspondence between the bodily gestures of a fifteenth-century Madonna and the astrological representation of the *facies* of the Virgin, but it would be absurd to claim that such a comparison could be elevated into a judgment about the meaning of a whole period.

The glorious myth of a rebirth, of a light which shattered the darkness, of a return of the ancient world, has great polemical strength. But as such it is not essentially linked to any special content. It stresses the fact that there was a new soul, a new form, a new way of looking at things and, above all, it emphasises that this new birth made man conscious of himself in a new way. The ancient world, classical antiquity, which as a result of this new birth had come to be regarded with much nostalgia, came now to be loved and cherished in a completely new manner. There is no denying that the ancient world had been known and loved in the middle ages as well. The ancient gods peopled the dreams of the anchorites and appeared to them as tempters, and at times they turned up in the old places to demand solemn sacrifices from the people. We have all read about the rages of Gunzone and the dreams of Vilgardo da Ravenna. They are full of classical scenes and in some of them people are invited to nothing less than an apostasy of the Christian gods and a return to pagan rites. We know of countless verses that are full of a profound love for ancient Rome, and Dante allowed the ancient poets to intrude into the economy of sacred history. He even brought in the ancient gods, turned demons, and made them live in the caves of hell.

Humanism, however, though full of love for Vergil and Cicero, no longer accepted Vergil as a prophet, and if humanists had faith in him, it was a completely new kind of faith. They believed in him in the sense that one believes in every human being who partakes of the light of truth. In this sense, the humanists were very far from worshipping the ancient gods—so much so that at times they gave the impression of not even believing in the new ones. The humanist's passion for the ancient world was no longer based on a barbarous confusion of his own culture with that of the ancient world. On the contrary his attitude was one of critical detachment. He saw the ancient world in historical dimensions and contemplated it as something which was situated in the august temple of the past. The myth of Renaissance paganism may have a certain justification for the purposes of argument; perhaps it can even be supported by reference to one of the decadent writers. But only historians lacking in wisdom can uphold it. As soon as we start to study the profound seriousness of humanistic philology, the myth is exploded. Gentile well observed that philology was the essential feature of the culture of humanism. By philology is meant a study so rich and complex that it includes a complete critical survey of the totality of man. It was not a pseudo-philosophy put forward by people who were not philosophers to use in their fight against genuine philosophy. It was a true, new, and serious philosophy. It amounted to both a restoration and a discovery of antiquity. But for this very reason it implied that antiquity was taken as something other, as something completely distinct from the thought of the humanists who did the discovering. The discovery was the result of laborious reconstruction; and for this reason antiquity was no longer seen as part of contemporary life. Antiquity, therefore, came to be defined as something that confronted the humanists. Its discovery was the discovery of an object which had to be placed into a valid relationship with the people who discovered it. The humanists thus found themselves *vis-à-vis* a historical past that was very different from their own world. It was precisely in this field of philosophy that there took place the conscious detachment from the past of which the humanists were so proud. It was a critic's detachment. The humanist wanted to learn from the classics not because he imagined that he shared a world with them but in order to define his own position as distinct from theirs. For this reason there arose a veritable gulf between those people who had loved the ancients because they thought they shared a common culture with them and the people who now realised that antiquity was something that had to be restored. The former, to make their belief come true, had often been forced to do violence—loving violence—to antiquity; and the latter sought to restore it with a passion for accuracy which bordered on pedantry. Thus a whole world closed up; and it was rediscovered at the very point where it was most closed. The face of ancient culture could no longer be simply reinterpreted. It had become once and for all part of history. It had ceased to be part of people's lives and had to be contemplated instead as a historical truth. There was detachment; and as a result of this detachment a classical author ceased to be part of me and I began to define my own identity as something different from him. I found my own identity by discovering his. The Renaissance myth of ancient civilisation was based upon a definition of the character of that civilisation. And in defining that character the Renaissance reduced that civilisation to something dead. There was not much of a break between antiquity and the middle ages—certainly less of a break than there was between the middle ages and the Renaissance. For it was precisely the Renaissance, or better, humanistic philology which made people conscious of the fact that there had been a break. It was here that the most important requirement of our culture came to the fore. We had to define our own identity by defining the identity of another civilisation. Thus we had to acquire a sense of history and a sense of time. We had to learn to see both history and time as the dimensions proper to the life of man. We had to abandon for good the idea that the world was solid and fixed, that it exhibited a graduated order and a permanent hierarchy —in short, that it was something definitive. We had to give up the notion that the world was a cosmos which could be contemplated, indifferent to the passage of time, secure in eternity and forever rotating in continuing circles. This old reality had been supposed to be utterly solid and to have a timeless subsistence—so much so that its very solidity had crushed all prophets of man's liberation. It had led instead to the grand manner of medieval speculation and to the diabolical temptation to absorb the disquietening Christian message into the security of the Aristotelian world.

From Petrarch onwards, humanism took up an entirely different position. A genuinely fruitful renewal, it sought a way out of an insoluble problem, in the areas of poetry and philology, ethics and politics. In the end it even sought a new way in a field which might appear hostile to humanism but which was nevertheless intimately connected with it: the field of the arts which godlessly attempted to change and subvert the world. Philology and poetry, understood in the sense of Vico, gave birth to the new philosophy.

THE IDEAL CITY

❡ In the manuscript B of the Institute of France, one will suddenly be struck (16 *r*-15 *v*) by an elegant sketch of buildings and streets flanked by colonnades. The caption, in Leonardo's rapid strokes and lapidary style, describes the image of the ideal city. It is built near the sea or along a river for the sake of health and cleanliness and constructed on two levels, linked by steps. One can walk through the whole of the upper level without having to descend to the lower one and vice versa. The traffic of wagons and beasts of burden will be confined to the lower level where the shops are also situated and where all trade will take place: ". . . one house must turn its back upon another and the lower street must run between the two."[1]

The minute particulars mentioned by Leonardo precisely define the purposes of the two levels of the city and emphasise the distinction between the classes. On the upper level there are the "gentlemen." On the lower level, according to the usage established in the *Codice Atlantico* (65 vb), "the rabble." On the whole

---

[1] Leonardo da Vinci, *Manuscrit B de l'Institute de France*, Grenoble, 1960, pp. 47–49.

in this famous project one is impressed by the prevalence of aesthetic preoccupations, which, nevertheless, are not altogether unconnected with a political conception of the city. In fact, the aesthetic preoccupations are part and parcel of the political conceptions. In the *Codice Atlantico* Leonardo offered advice to Ludovico Moro for making Milan beautiful. But here too the advice turns upon a beauty conceived in terms of functionality. As in all such plans for cities, the dominant thoughts are hygienic ones. The author is preoccupied with an adequate supply of water and with an even distribution of people in houses and wards to avoid overcrowding, which is not only dangerous to public health but also a threat to law and order.

The intention was to substitute for the medieval city, grown haphazardly and without order and with buildings heaped along narrow and tortuous streets, a new city, planned according to a rational design. Complex and contradictory arrangements were to be replaced by organically articulate order. For the point had been reached when a society, fully matured, had become conscious of itself, and reflected about its own structure and sought suggestions for the future from its own past, weighing experience and reason against the lessons of history.

It is not difficult to see that the original inspiration for such plans was derived from classical texts, which were read either in the original or in some other form and were freely elaborated upon by politicians and architects in their attempts to design the ideal city of the Renaissance. Leonardo's plan was to divide the city into two parts. There was to be the lower part where work and the services, including the most humble, were to be concentrated. Only if one bears this in mind can one understand that the dominant idea, over and above Vitruvius, was the Platonic correspondence between state and man, between the parts of the body and the soul, and the various classes

The plan of the city had to reflect the hierarchy of governors and workers. This does not mean that Leonardo ought to be considered a conventional Platonist. But it is true that Plato's *Republic*, translated so many times during the fifteenth century both in Florence and Milan, was bound to make its impact upon the workshop of an artist of genius. There will be occasion to speak of Leonardo's Platonism—but in a different sense and in a different connection. Here I merely wish to call attention in these projects for an ideal city to the strict connection between political structure and architectural structure, and to the link beween the body and soul of the new *polis*, at whose core it is never difficult to spot the profile of the ancient *polis*. The ideal state of which people spoke was always the city-state or the *res publica* which in its architectural form objectified an economic and political structure assimilated to the image of man as defined by humanism. All these projects give a rational definition of the true nature of man in terms of a particular historical experience.

In discussing the architects and town-planners of the Renaissance, from Alberti to Leonardo, scholars have too often spoken of the tyranny of aesthetics and of a divorce of beauty from functionality, of the dominion of rhetoric over concrete political, economic, and social considerations. But the truth is that more often one finds in these men a special way of understanding and of transforming functionality. In his design for Milan Leonardo makes explicit reference to beauty; but this beauty coincides completely with a functionality represented by rational form. The city must be made to the measure of man. And man at the point of his highest development is "a gentleman," who lives both in light and in harmony. For this reason, the buildings, the streets, and all the other places must adjust themselves to a human measure. Leonardo's design, far from being a fantastic plan, was firmly based upon the realistic aspirations

of the Italian city-state. It was meant to shape at least
one of them—Milan—according to a general type
answering to the rationale which pulsates in the bosom
of Nature. Hence there is a certain necessity inherent
in this type. Indeed, if one examines the general tone
of Alberti's and Leonardo's philosophy of nature over
and above their preoccupation with town-planning
and architecture one will find a great many similarities between these two artists—similarities which concern their idea of *logoi*, of seminal reasons, of immanent mathematical laws which man discovers a
the foundation of being. Man's own works and crea
tions are to be grafted upon natural things; though
new and original, these works must rely upon natura
necessities and conform to the rational network o
the universe. They express it and give substance to it
In other words, human reason is not supposed to
fight against hostile natural forces. Its task, rather, i
to co-ordinate them, by means of a body of law
which is the expression of a fully integrated tota
legislation. Free human activity is subject to thi
universal legislation and never can work against it
Man and nature, human reason and natural law, com
plement one another. The ideal city, therefore, is a
one and the same time both a rational city and
natural city. It is a city built by reason according to
a human measure; but it is also a city which corre
sponds perfectly to the nature of man.

These attitudes had been shaped a long time ago
They had first taken form when in the evolution o
the Italian city-state people had realised the need fo
a political organisation and, with that organisation, fo
an architectural reconstruction capable of taking car
of new developments. These developments had bee
brought about by the sheer vigour of conflicting force
as well as by the conscious effort of people who ha
shaped and perfected a sophisticated culture. There i
no denying that problems of town planning wer
always connected with problems of politics, such a

the constitution, the magistracy and taxation. Similarly one can never forget the remarkable suddenness with which a great number of Italian cities had begun to build walls. All the time people were intent upon connecting the problem of the sudden increase in the size of populations with the redistribution of them according to a rational plan and their fundamental preoccupations were three: public health, internal security, defence against foreign attacks and, hence, precautions in case of war or siege. We can observe not only the plans for city walls and the discussion about the suitability of building towns along rivers or near the sea, in plains or on mountains, but also an incessant preoccupation with the possibility of epidemics, popular riots, struggles for power, sieges, sacks, and, last but not least, hunger. For these reasons all the treatises on town planning ended up being treatises on politics. They emphasised the search for a rationalisation of the city on the legislative as well as on the architectural level. Cities were made for men, and therefore had to be made to the measure of men. Looked at from another angle such rationalisation was also a harmonisation. It was a search for a balance which corresponded to a conception of a life freer and more beautiful than had been known in the past. It would, however, be inexact to say that the prime motive of such plans and efforts was an aesthetic one, if we take the word "aesthetic" in its modern meaning.

It is indeed worth noting how much in the writing of all kinds of authors considerations of town planning converge with reflections on politics and society. One has no difficulty in finding in Florentine texts of the late fourteenth century and the beginning of the fifteenth century comparisons between the institutions of a republic and its buildings. Such comparisons are especially explicit in regard to Florence, which was considered something of an ideal type of

city. The Palace of the *Signori* and the cathedral
become more than symbols: they are taken as tangible expressions of the organisation of power. It is
equally important that the writings of the age of humanism indicate that the ideal form of the political
organisation of a city, of a city-state, is to be found in
a declared opposition to the great unitary organisms
of the ancient world and of the middle ages, the
Roman Empire, the Germanic Empire, and the Italian
Kingdom. And eventually the attack turned even
against the pretension of the Church of Rome. It is
clear that the whole history of the struggle for urban
autonomy has been brought to bear on this question
of the defence of the city as an ideal form of political
organisation; and this defence is the expression of
the desire for independence from the all too frequent
interference by papal and imperial power. At the
same time it is certain that in the age of humanism it
was easy to find an inspiration for this line of argument in ancient Greek treatises. The Florentine
Chancellor, Leonardo Bruni, who at the beginning
of the fifteenth century translated Aristotle's *Politics*
came across the famous passage (1326b) in which it
is laid down that if one wishes to have efficient magistrates and good order, "the citizens should be personally well acquainted with one another. For if they
do not know each other, the election of officials will
be carried out badly and irrational sentence will be
imposed." "Too large a crowd," Bruni translated
"cannot be turned into a civic community." Or at
least not into a city capable of living well as a civic
society.[2] In his eyes Plato's *Republic* had had much
the same projection. Over a wider area unity can
be produced only by alliances between cities. It
can certainly never result from the suppression of
cities by large-scale political organisations. Thus
when people in the fifteenth century made use of the

---

[2] Aristotle, *Opera*, III, Venetiis apud Iunctas, 1574, 293 L

Roman experience, they looked to the republican rather than to the imperial era of Roman history, not only in regard to domestic affairs, but also with the conviction that in the age of republicanism cities had preserved their autonomy because they had been able to develop without too many obstacles.

Bruni, Chancellor as well as historian of Florence, was one of the first humanists to translate Plato and Aristotle. He also made a profound study of the Florentine constitution. In his *History of the Florentine People* he argued against any exaggerated notion of the value of imperial Rome and maintained that Roman power and the centralising tendency of the Roman state had had a deadening effect upon the life of the cities, their trade and their culture. His opposition to great states and to empires allowed no exception for Rome. Rome, to him, was the octopus which had strangled every other centre.[3]

There was probably no other author in the fifteenth century who praised the small state, the *Kleinstaat*, with the eloquence of Bruni. Werner Kaegi, in his particularly good discussion of the small state, makes many a reference to the Italian cities of the Renaissance, but he does not mention the Florentine Chancellor, even though he uses nearly the same words when he describes the people's secret joy at the news of the cessation of the Roman administrative system. "People felt," he exclaims, "greatly relieved, when they were freed from the crushing glory of the Roman name and could turn back to a mode of life more primitive but more healthy, that is, to their own city and their own province."[4]

At one point, Bruni, although he was probably the

---

[3] L. Bruni, *Historiae*, E. Santini, ed., *Rerum Italicarum Scriptores*, XIX, 3, Città di Castello, 1914, p. 7.

[4] W. Kaegi, *Meditazioni storiche*, D. Cantimori, ed., Bari, 1960, p. 7.

most astute theoretician and the most elegant historian of the city-state, did not hesitate to turn history into propaganda and theoretical reflection into a concrete project in his fight against the myth of Rome. At that moment Florence and her constitution became to him the ideal prototype of the just city, well ordered, harmonious and beautiful, ruled by *taxis* and *cosmos*. His *Laudatio Florentinae Urbis* was composed at the beginning of the century on the model of the *Panathenaikos* of Elio Aristide. It contained images which are reminiscent of the *Laws* of Plato. It is not only a noteworthy example of the imitation of classical models which was all the rage but also a specific political treatise. The central part of the treatise argues that liberty is possible only in the safekeeping of civic autonomy, i.e. in the small state. It is well known that Leonardo Bruni wrote immediately after Florence's conflict with Gian Galeazzo Sforza, who had wanted to establish a grand unitary dominion over Italy under Milanese hegemony. Florence had risen to defend her republican liberty against a unification which would leave enslaved the Italian cities to the "tyrant." Florence had thus vindicated pluralism against unity. Bruni took up an ancient theme when he wrote that a city, in order to be free, must be just; "With all diligence one has to see to it that sacred justice reigns supreme, for without it no city can exist." His profile of the just and free state—the two features are complementary—is the profile of a rational state in which order, functions, magistrates, powers, and all groups are distinct from one another, though co-ordinated. "In (Florence) there is nothing disorderly, nothing improper, nothing without reason or cause. Everything has its place. And this not only happens to be so, but it is also both convenient and necessary." The highest power is entrusted to nine citizens, and they are changed every two months. Multiple organs of execution and control, the separa-

tion of powers, preserve the republic from tyranny.
At the same time, the state seeks, in its punishments
as well as in its imposts, that is, in the administration
of criminal justice as well as in the imposition of
taxes, to realise a distributive justice. Thus it is able to
correct the laws of nature and can intervene as
required against those who are too powerful and in
favour of those who are too weak. It can arbitrate in
the clash between the poor and the rich and assume
the protection of the poor and the miserable. "Hence
there is a certain equality: the more powerful citizens
are defended by their own power and the lesser
citizens, by the Republic."[5]

Bruni was referring in an idealised manner to the
internal affairs of the Florentine Republic. From the
time of the *Ordinamenti di Giustizia* (1293) to the
rebellion of the *Ciompi* (1378) the lower classes had
gained power, while the position of the new bourgeoisie of the city had become consolidated. The
Ordinamenti had differentiated between the members
of the lower classes and the knights, and had, in fact,
reserved especially hard punishments for those knights
who attacked members of the lower classes or made
attempts upon the security of the state. Bruni thought
of these differences in treatment as some kind of
special reparation that the justice of the state could
make in order to compensate for the lack of natural
justice and equality. "Whoever you are, if you are
rich you are not a friend of the poor, no matter how
much you pretend to be." With these words Ser
Piero Cennini, a notary, introduced in 1480 a measure
of graduated taxation. He wanted to remind people,
though by that time for purely formal and rhetorical
reasons, of the old principles of distributive justice.

---

[5] L. Bruni, *Le vere lodi de la inclita et gloriosa città di
Firenze*, tr. by Frate Lazzaro da Padova, Florence, 1899,
passim.

But a few years later, with reference to the graduated tax of 1494 which hit the wealthy property owners very hard, Guicciardini observed with bitterness: "This measure thus proposed, met with much favourable support in spite of the fact that it was most unjust and caused damage to the public; for it is useful to the city to maintain wealth, even though each wealthy man thinks only of himself. It found favour with the poor. There had to be an impost and they wanted this one rather than another, for this one did not hurt them."[6] We are by now in the Florence of Savonarola, struck by the prophetic announcement of radical political and religious renewal. Nevertheless, the level on which people were thinking was still the level of the small, just city in which all social inequalities were remedied by the provisions of rational laws which led to a well-measured egalitarianism in the community.

According to Bruni architectural planning must correspond to political and social structure. The city is supposed to stretch along the banks of a river. He was propounding the constant theme of Renaissance town-planning. Even as a ship must have the captain in the centre, so the city is to have the Palace of the *Signori* and the temple, at the centre. The city is to be divided rationally: the houses are to be oriented in such a way as to have rooms for winter and rooms for summer and they are to be built "beautifully and precisely" along streets which lead towards the hills and the suburbs among which the city proper gradually loses itself, as if there were a series of concentric circles, each larger than the one before. The design is neat and precise. The image is that of Elio Aristide. But behind it there hovers an image substantially identical with that drawn in the sixth book of Plato's

---

[6] G. Canestrini, *La scienza e l'arte di stato desunta dagli atti ufficiali della Republica fiorentina e die Medici*, I, *L'imposta nella ricchezza mobile e immobile*, Florence, 1862, p. 265.

Laws in which, too, there are to be concentric circles around the *agora* and the public buildings.[7]

Leonardo Bruni's work is so important because his Ideal city, so full of echoes of Plato, is not a work of fantasy, divorced from reality, but tends to identify itself with an actually existing city. He merely idealises and corrects some of its features according to a higher rationality. He is, of course, thinking of Florence. Viewed in the framework of her history, Florence seemed destined to realise the rational state understood as the state natural to man. Leonardo Bruni is no Rousseau. But in his political and historical writings Florence plays the role played by Geneva in the pages of Rousseau. Rousseau described his state, thinking of his native Geneva. In turn, he saw Geneva through the glasses of his own political ideal. Leonardo Bruni read his ancient Greeks and thought of Florence and came to look upon Florence through the pages of the political writings of Plato and Aristotle. It has often been said of both the *Laudatio* and the *Historiae* that they are rhetorical writings. But this is an ambiguous term. They are really political writings in which a definite city-state is held up as the ideal of human communal life, as the realisation of a social order based upon rational principles. The perfect city, the arch-city, in its buildings as well as in its institutions, does not exist outside this world, in heaven or in the land of Utopia. It is located on earth, even though not yet fully finished. If one surveys the literature of the fifteenth century and compares it with the literature of the following century, one will discover that instead of Utopias it contains "praises" of actual cities (of Florence, Venice, Milan); histories or descriptions of specific constitutions held up as examples; reflections upon constitutions to be imitated by others. In this fifteenth-century literature there is not only no longing for

---

[7] *Laws*, 788 c.

celestial and other imaginary cities but also no attempt
to seek a foundation for civic life in religion as Pletho
was to do when he propounded his solar cult—and
Pletho was a thinker who was well acquainted with
the work of Bruni.

We ought to compare Bruni's position with that of
Dante Alighieri, whom he loved. Bruni wrote a life
of Dante and held him up as the model of a good
citizen. But a comparison of these two authors shows
how far apart from each other they actually were
and how radically the whole situation in Florence
had been transformed in little more than a century.
To Dante, the ideal Florence is the Florence of
Cacciaguida, the distant vision of a patriarchal past.
This city is enclosed in its old walls, regulated by
an austere discipline. Dante's vision is dominated by a
rigid moralism, by a rejection of the present, and by
an archaic myth which stands in strong contrast to
contemporary life, its trade, its wealth, and its culture
in all its many aspects. Dante saw his *Monarchy* as a
universal empire which reproduced that of Augustus
and represented the myth of Rome, but symmetrically
opposite to this walled-in city. The relations between
the empire he imagined and the church were difficult,
because he viewed them in terms of the past, innocent
of the rebirth of nations. He was caught in the blind
alley of the unresolved conflicts between the spiritual
and the temporal. It was as if he were dreaming far-
away from actual historical conditions in a climate
singularly remote from facts. Forced to address himself to one single question, to the question of the
relations between church and state, Dante seems to
have been completely oblivious of any power other
than the single imperial one. And what is more he
saw this power only in the vaguest terms and conceived it as some kind of fantastic conjunction of
Augustus and the Emperors of the House of Swabia.
Dante's book is completely dominated by the conflict
between the universalism of empire and the universal-

ism of the Roman Catholic Church. It ignores and
even opposes the blossoming of the new city-state and
the importance of the new force of the bourgeoisie.
It does not take into account the progress of the
common people and attributes every evil to the dis-
order caused by the temporal pretensions of the
church or of spiritual power in general. For this
reason, Dante's *Monarchia* acquits itself of its task
entirely within the limits of his opposition to the
church, i.e. his arguments are always critical and
never constructive. "Perfect like an architect's design," Gilson wrote in his *Les métamorphoses de la
cité de Dieu*, "Dante's solution remains somewhat
indefinite . . . especially when it comes to a discussion
of the means for translating it into practice." Gilson
nevertheless adds: "We ought not to blame him.
There is no doubt that, if questioned, he would have
replied that he was a philosopher charged with the
solution of a philosophical problem, and that he could
not hold himself responsible for the practical conditions required for the realisation of the solution he
proposed. The practical realisation of the plan was
the Emperor's job."

Gilson tells us at the same time that unfortunately
it is precisely as a philosopher that Dante is wrong;
"In spite of the fact that his image of the empire
claims to be modelled on the Rome of Augustus, his
conception of monarchy is nothing but a temporal
version of that spiritual society which is the church."
Dante is therefore wrong in believing that "unaided
natural reason is capable of bringing about agreement
and co-operation among all men through the sheer
truth of one single philosophical system." Gilson insists that the development of human reason was
destined to take a dangerous twist. He thinks that the
pluralism characteristic of the modern age is the
"worst philosophical chaos the world has ever
known." At the same time, if we are to follow Gilson,
Dante was also mistaken in his conception of the

relationship between the temporal and the spiritual: "the temporal and political order is happier and wiser when it accepts the spiritual and religious jurisdiction of the church. Even though papal authority, when it extends to the political field, may be a direct authority, it is never either temporal or political in the accepted sense of these terms." As a result, Dante's conception of a Roman monarchy in which there is no trace of church, Christianity, or the City of God is "the first modern expression of the idea of a single temporal society of the whole of mankind."[8]

Leaving out the question of Dante's modernity, it is certain that his thoughts moved on a level which was opposed to the political thought and the political realities of the fourteenth and fifteenth centuries. His *Monarchia*, the quintessence of his imperial dream and of his hatred of the papacy, is diametrically opposed in its universalism and its unitary ideal to the city-states which were taking shape and whose destiny would completely transcend the realm of his preoccupations. One must not be deceived by his anti-papal polemics. The city-state which was about to be born was not only a complete break with Dante's conception of a universal monarchy; it was also a form of communal life to which the religious battles so dear to Dante were altogether foreign. The city-state lived in and through pluralism. It established rationality through the co-ordination of rational human beings. It saw the secret of liberty and peace in the balance between autonomous human beings. It built its cathedral by the side of the Palace of the *Signori*, of the schools and the banks, inside the civic circle. It sought to define the conditions for communal life on a mundane level, the only level it was interested in. In such a city-state the problems of laicisation were problems of co-ordination and collab-

---

[8] E. Gilson, *Les métamorphoses de la cité de Dieu*, Louvain-Paris, 1952, p. 150ff.

oration in temporal concerns and had nothing to do with the question of heresy or lack of piety. For these reasons the fifteenth-century Italian city-state did not pursue radical religious programs nor did it place religion in the centre of the scheme of things even though occasionally it sought to bring about a confrontation between conflicting conceptions. The theoreticians of the city-state therefore showed no longing for the solar cult of Pletho or for the solar cities of Campanella. As they were intent upon seeking the best kind of political constitution, they kept their eyes firmly fixed upon very concrete political, social, and economic problems and found themselves in opposition to the myths of the past as well as to the dreams of the "new age." They killed the last remnants of myth when they sought to detect the origins of Florence in Etruria and rejected the idea that Florence had been founded by the Romans. Similar historical revisions were made in other cities. As a result of such revisions the unification of Italy under Rome came to be looked upon as something temporary and unfortunate. Bruni rejoiced in the trade, the wealth, and the expansion of the cities. He was grateful because the cities could breathe outside the limits of the ancient walls and the confines of ruined empires. Hence he considered the whole conception of Dante's *Monarchia* as something utterly alien and distant. Modern thinkers were aware that their societies stemmed from the autonomy of the small states and the co-ordination of various orders, just as on the theoretical level they defended pluralistic doctrines and points of view. They understood the parallelism between the fall of ancient political orders and the fall of ancient conceptions of the world. This age of revolutions was bound to emphasise the value of pluralism in every field. People who lived through the revolution were bound to be republicans; and even if on their horizon there happened to survive an odd trace of monarchical authority, such a trace was always a constitutional sovereign who reigned but did not govern.

In truth, in the fifteenth century the process of the dissolution of ancient structures had already reached its limit and we find therefore an increasingly clear consciousness of new solutions for changed conditions. In many Italian cities the new groups of citizens who had achieved power sought to consolidate it in adequate forms and at the same time were trying to reorganise the cities according to plans sensitive to the problems posed by commerce, industry, and banking as well as by administration. It is no accident that in many ancient communal cities the centre was gradually being shifted to the palaces of the great bankers in which the true political captains were living. In Florence, for instance, the centre moved from the market-place in front of the Palace of the *Signori* to the splendid palace of the Medici, the *Casa Medici*, a new architectural expression of a new function.

In such a situation all talk about a return to the past in the guise of a longing for a myth, or any hope for a future age in the guise of a longing for an imaginary perfection to be reached at the end of all time, was bound to lose its meaning. The rational task in hand—and that is the task of which we are speaking—intended to make use of classical theories as useful supports and as suggestions for a condition which had not yet found a sufficiently systematic treatment of its own. In other words, in the fifteenth century, the so-called myth of the ancient world was not yet a myth; and the Platonic Republic was not used as a utopia. Just as in physics Archimedes was considered more actual and more modern than Buridano, both Vitruvius and Plato appeared more relevant and modern than the theoreticians of the middle ages. It was held that to imitate ancient cities, in town planning as well as in political constitutions, was to obey both reason and nature. In his *Art of War* Machiavelli said quite clearly that what seemed a dedication to "things dead" was in reality a vital task. And Fabrizio Colonna wrote that in a modern city "where there was something worthwhile," the life and the order of the Roman Republic were a valid prescription. The ideal city, in its buildings as well as in its institutions, is a rational city. Such rational cities were described and realised by the Greeks, and the Italian city-state must endeavour to reproduce that ancient type. When a learned Byzantine scholar, in the middle of the fifteenth century, offered a translation of Plato's *Laws* to one of the Senators of Venice, he observed that in Venice the designs of the ancient philosophers had been put into practise. Similar eulogies of Florence and Venice emphasised that the real perfection of the ancient city-state had been reborn: these ancient cities were cities which had actually existed and could return to life. In the fifteenth century we find once more a great confidence in the power and virtue of man. This confidence did away with the hankering after models supposed to have existed in a legendary past or for a future which was to take place outside history. And thus this confidence took the place of myth, utopia, and apocalypse. Small power was accorded to luck and fortune, and insofar as either existed at all, it was held that they could be overcome by cleverness and prudent calculation. One can go further: given the confidence that it was possible to build a city according to reason as the ancients had done, the problem was not so much how this was to be done as to what had caused decadence. How is it, people were prone to ask, that an edifice constructed according to all the rules of art can crumble? And Coluccio Salutati had asked himself how the Palace of the *Signori* in Florence, so rationally perfect, could ever break up.

All in all, and it is important to emphasise this, the climate of opinion which made Plato's *Republic* one of the most popular of the ancient books was not a climate of unrealistic speculation but of practical plans. There was no room for the planning of imaginary cities, but only for the construction of real ones. It may be true that one of the reasons for the popularity of Plato was the interest people had in the idea of a hierarchical society with well-defined classes. The parallel with Venice was only too obvious. But in spite of this, the feature which made the greatest impression was the conception of the rationality of the just state, the possibility of reaching some kind of concord through a rational order which could harmonise all opposed interests. It is worth repeating that at the centre of all these new cities there stood the symbol of *iustitia*. Werner Kaegi has reminded us that it was "present everywhere, in hundreds of images, on fountains and gates, on the paintings in council chambers and on the portals of the cathedrals, in the prefaces to the civic law books and the preambles to public statutes. It was truly both the vital spirit and the meaning of the city."[9] According to Giannozzo Manetti, in Florence, when the *gonfaloniere* took up his office, he had to sing the praises of *Justice* in public, to discourse about its essence and to provide an interpretation of it.

There was something else in the manner in which Plato's *Republic* was taken up. There was the idea that justice is capable of fitting the human order into the natural order and that human law can be derived from the laws of nature. The middle ages, right down to the fourteenth century, had read the *Timaeos*, the book about natural justice and the law which regulates nature and governs the world. But when Emanuel Chysoloras at the dawn of the fifteenth century introduced Latin-speaking people to Plato's *Republic*, it was discovered that the notion of civil justice pointed to the possibility of extending geomet-

---

[9] W. Kaegi, *op cit.*, p. 20.

rical order to human societies. Thinking of Leonardo, one can see that at the very point that the new science of nature emerged, there also emerged the longing for a scientific construction of the city either according to mathematics or to reason.

"The wise man will triumph over the stars." This famous motto of astrology is frequently to be found in fifteenth-century writings intended to increase the stature of man. It expresses the conviction that man, provided he takes care, can evade even the fate imposed by the stars. But it also expresses the belief that only those with a scientific outlook such as described by the architect Francesco di Giorgio Martini can become the masters of matter and organise their community life. Thus the Platonic gulf between the sage and the sovereign had to be abandoned. The motto dear to the Renaissance was: "An illiterate king is a crowned ass." It should be taken as a homage to the active intellect and as a tribute to the belief that science is necessary for everything. In a certain sense, the connection between the physical city, i.e. between the architecture of the city, and the city in its moral and civic sense is a tangible expression of the continuity between nature and civic life, and between the laws of nature and civil laws. Thus several old ideas, common to Cicero and Vitruvius, came to be charged with a new meaning.

A comparative study of the political literature and the works by technical architects and town-planners of the fifteenth century is bound to be rewarding. On the one hand we have Uberto Decembrio who had together with Chrysoloras translated Plato's *Republic* and who also wrote a number of political dialogues in which he discussed the affairs of the state of the Visconti in terms of Plato's masterpiece. On the other side we have Filarete, a Florentine who had gone to live in Lombardy. He was the architect of the Hospital of Milan and also produced an outline of an imaginary city called Sforzinda which expressed his idea of a perfect city.[10]

The city envisaged by Alberti was, as has been observed, neither medieval nor preromantic. It was dominated by the preoccupation with a Platonic justice, with its neat divisions of classes, organised inside walls which enclose "one circle inside another." It was to be one city inside another, ordered like a series of concentric circles. According to Leonardo the order was based upon plains: on the upper plain, by the light of truth and the sun, the gentlemen, the governors; and down below, the workers, "the crowd of paupers." According to Alberti, inside one of the walls, built high and proud, fortified with towers and surrounded by a moat like a real fortress, there were the merchants and the grocers, butchers, and cooks. These particular walls were supposed to tower high above the roofs of the buildings of private citizens.[11]

To be precise, Alberti drew a distinction between the new principalities and the kingdoms on one side and the free republics on the other. The new principalities ought to cling to the mountains and, being full of fear and suspicion, seek to defend themselves. But the free people may live in the comfortable cities of the plains. Leaving this difference aside, Alberti's city was designed to emphasise class distinctions and to express a precise political structure in terms of walls and buildings. In this way, to be an architect became synonymous with being a governor and co-ordinator of all civic activities. Freely adapting an Aristotelian expression, Alberti thought of architecture as the art of all arts, as the art which unifies and governs all the others. The science of town-planning

---

[10] U. Decembrio, *De re publica*, Milan, Bibl. Ambros., B 123 sup., F. 8off.; A. Averlino Filarete, *Tractat über die Baukunst*, abridged edition by W. von Oettingen, Wien, 1896.

[11] L. B. Alberti, *Della architettura libri dieci* (trans. by Cosimo Bartoli), Milan, 1833, pp. 135–36.

was thus not only connected with politics but was identified as politics and gave exemplary expression to it. "I will call an architect him who knows both in mind and soul to divide with the help of marvellous reason and rule. An architect is a man who knows how to bring to conclusion all those things which, through movement and weight, conjunction and massing of bodies can well be accommodated with dignity to the use of man. In order to be able to accomplish all this, it is necessary that he should be conversant with the best and the most excellent things, and that he should have made them his own."

If one studies more closely than is usually the case the writings of town-planners, military technicians, and of artists and craftsmen in general, one will come across in those that are interested in science the idea that practical knowledge is directed towards constructions and buildings for public utility and civic use. This kind of knowledge was supposed to be universal and capable of embracing the whole body of the sciences and the arts. Just as in a city all the works of man in society are united and given practical expression so the man who builds and plans the city embodies the totality of all human faculties. Thus Ghiberti demanded that the artisan ought to know everything and Leonardo wanted his painter to be possessed of a universal science. Leon Battista Alberti even arrived at the notion that man is a builder by nature and that he is most human when he is an architect: "One can see from many things how much delight men derive from thinking and talking about building and how deeply ingrained it is in the soul of man. One learns this particularly from the fact that one will never find anybody, provided there is an opportunity, who does not have in himself a certain inclination to build something. And if there is anybody who has discovered in his mind something to do with building, he will speak up voluntarily and offer

it for the use of other men as if he had been forced
to do so by nature."[12]

There is no doubt that to Alberti the expression
"to build" has a very wide meaning. In his terminol-
ogy a man who constructs churches and fortifications
regulates rivers and builds dikes and harbours, a man
who devises methods for the purification of water
or who makes ships and manufactures artillery for
warfare, is a builder. In Alberti's mind there is no
difference between the circulation of commercial
goods and the circulation of ideas. There is no difference between "victuals, spices, jewels, news and
pieces of knowledge for they are all things useful to
the health and goodness of life." A city in its physical
being, in its buildings, is the civic community made
real and concrete and fully manifest. For this reason
the architect is the universal man. Or, if one prefers
the governor becomes architect and the politician a
theoretician of architecture precisely at the point that
science becomes practical and is joined to political
wisdom. It is therefore impossible to understand the
political ideas of the fifteenth century without taking
into account the builders of cities. They cannot be
understood without Cosimo's obsessive building of
walls, without the architectural projects of Nicholas
V, without remembering that a city was taken to
have changed its appearance because it had changed
its activity; for with this change in activity, the centre
of the city had been dislodged and all social relations
together with the mode of life, altered. Town-planners and their clients not only responded to demands
but frequently imposed their own plans "according
to the rationality of architecture," as Francesco di
Giorgio was wont to say. "Rationality" here meant
that one had to build living quarters that were "in
good proportion and delightful . . . of pleasant appearance and attractive." They had to surround the

---

[12] L. B. Alberti, *Della architettura*, p. xxi.

city square and the market, which was compared to the man's battlefield. The whole city had to be made to the measure of man. "It is the body of man, better organised than any other and as it is perfect it is proper that every other building should be constructed in his image."[13] It is not surprising that in such a climate of thought the most impressive image of the ideal city should have been put forward by an architect. Filarete, also known as Antonio Averlino, is a case in point. He was born in Florence in 1400. Between the years 1460 and 1464 he composed the twenty-five books of his *Treatise on Architecture*. Though dedicated to Sforza, a splendidly illustrated copy was presented to Piero de' Medici. It is still preserved in the National Library of Florence.[14]

According to Filarete, man has the natural inclination to build. Building is like generating: "Building is a voluptuous pleasure, as when a man is in love." Man the maker of artifacts expresses his primary nature in the city. All building is done in the image of the builder and, like the builder, all building is something individual. "Thus I give you the building made in the form and likeness of man . . . You can never see a house or a building or any human habitation which is completely like any other in appearance, form or beauty . . ."

All the same, buildings have to be planned according to reason. Sforzinda, the *ville radieuse* of the Renaissance, is "beautiful, good, and perfect because of the course of nature." The various buildings respond organically to the needs of the citizens, to their government, their justice, education and the training of the artisans, to the requirements of defence, the curing of illnesses, and physical training. Each build-

---

[13] Francesco di Giorgio Martini, *Trattato d'architettura civile e militare*, C. Saluzzo ed., Turin, 1841, pp. 156–57, 191, 193.

[14] Ms. Naz. II, I, 40.

ing of Sforzinda translates one of these economic o
political requirements into stone. This conceptio
gives birth to a whole forest of buildings, all ordere
according to reason. And at the same time they cor
respond to a scintillating imagination, expressed b
Filarete in unique sketches. In these sketches, th
grandiose is executed with the same loving care a
every single detail: the college is there with everyon
of its small rooms; the prison, with everything neces
sary for torture. And with the elaboration of institu
tions there goes the abolition of capital punishmen
All summary punishments bear witness to the prevail
ing social equilibrium.

A recent historian has observed that Averlino wa
the first to conceive an organic plan for a whol
city. He added that when we pass from the individua
buildings to the whole, we pass from a consideratio
of what is possible to the planning of a utopia. Thu
when we contemplate the political structure o
Sforzinda, we will find "something like a commun
organism, with all the civic magistracies and th
rigid craft guilds. There is a patriarchal simplicity
austere costumes, and a profound sense of the collec
tive interest." But placed above it, something con
tradictory and useless, a Renaissance prince.[15] Fo
the most part this is only too true. There were repub
lican cities in a state of crisis, there were princes wh
founded new states, and there was the birth of whol
nations beyond the narrow confines of the city-stat
But the city-state, which was supposed to be th
masterpiece of rational organisation, burnt itself ou
internally and was suffocated from abroad. The ra
tional processes of the city-state were broken up an
overtaken by historical processes. In the midst of thes
delusions and defeats there arose prophecies, apoca
lyptic visions, evocations of primeval paradises an

---

[15] L. Firpo, "La città ideale del Filarette," in *Studi i
memoria di Gioele Solari*, Turin, p. 56.

dreams of solutions devoid of all reality. Thus we leave Sforzinda far behind and are given solar cities and imaginary republics instead.

The ideal city of the fifteenth-century treatises was a rational city. It was a real city, brought to a state of final perfection and developed according to its nature. It was a plan capable of realisation. It was always based on Florence or Venice or Milan but with the laws made perfect and the structures completed. It was a natural city, subject to the operation of the laws immanent in things. Without extremism, justice was derived from co-ordination and organisation. Justice was a problem capable of solution by wise discussions and by voluntary agreements and through equitable taxation. In Plato, one admired the rationality, the architecture, and the division of classes rather than the community of goods and women. In this way the ideal city was in its physical appearance as well as in its institutions a plan capable of realisation. It stemmed from the confidence that man had in himself, and this confidence was confirmed by countless ancient stories of ideal cities which had been realised. There had been Sparta and Athens, as now there were Florence and Venice. The problems were always the same: politics, town-planning, wisdom, justice. And it is important to note that in none of the writings, be they dialogues, histories, or eulogies, was there much room left for the great questions of religion.

For the ideal city of the fifteenth century was on this earth and must neither be compared to nor confused with the heavenly city. It was an individual entity. The primary condition for its own life consisted in autonomy, in the harmonious organisation of the crowd which composed it, and in the multiplicity of the crowd thus co-ordinated. In tracing the metamorphosis of the city of God in the fifteenth century Gilson considers only one text, the *De Pace Fidei* by Cusanus. He understands that that philosopher did not address himself to a religious problem at all, but to the problem of peace on earth and that he recognised the *de facto* existence of a large variety of beliefs and even legitimised this variety. There was no more talk "of one single and identical wisdom" but "the coexistence of different religions in the bosom of one common peace." On earth, "wisdom" must co-ordinate crowds and organise them.[16] Here again we find pluralism and harmony and above all the problem of human co-existence on earth.

All these arguments were derived from the humanists' confidence in man, in his reason, and in his capacity to build. The humanists considered him a *homo faber*, master of himself as well as of his destiny. If one peruses the literature of the fifteenth century one will be struck by the fact that it contains so many variations on the theme of destiny or *fortuna*. There are constant references to the idea that the sphere over which fortune reigns supreme is increasing and that one ought to distrust man's own strength. And above all one will find references to the insight that even the ideal states of antiquity were finally undone by *fortuna*, i.e. bad luck. Even Plato's Republic was destroyed by *tyche*, and the wise man, it was repeatedly said, is left to ponder the causes of the decline of Rome. Thus as the fifteenth century drew to a close we find a multiplication of prophecies, reflections on misfortunes and catastrophes as well as on redemption. The Florence of Savonarola, the new sacred city, the mystical heir of Jerusalem, was very far-away from the Florence of Leonardo Bruni. If it is true that Savonarola, when confronted with the concrete realities of politics, continued to believe in the perfection of the Venetian constitution, it is also true that he saw, at the end of time, the doom of divine justice, the relentless punishment of sin. The triumph of justice in a city,

---

[16] E. Gilson, *op. cit.*, pp. 180–81.

he held, was the work of wise governors; it is tied to the rhythm of sin and redemption, to divine intervention. The coming of the ideal city was thus linked with the prophecy of the "new age," of human regeneration and universal peace. It became part of the idea that the whole of the human race be united under one single shepherd. In this way the vision of a new Jerusalem, of a city of the sun and of a universal monarchy, replaced the older preoccupation with constitutions and orders of magistrates, taxes, and the size of streets and the height of buildings. Religious visions and the echoes of the prophecies of Abbot Joachim came to be the substitutes for rational discourse.

Machiavelli, with his experience and his knowledge of ancient history, was the companion of Leonardo. But for the rest, the sixteenth century bore witness to the Platonising exercises of Francesco Patrizi and the bizarre speculations about imaginary republics of Anton Francesco Doni. These speculations were designed to save, anachronistically, in the midst of invasions and the wars of empires, the appearance and illusion of the small city-state.[17] By that time, the actual reality consisted in a state of religious anxiety: among defeats and hopes, there existed the longing for a new age which was to free mankind from all servitude and carry it beyond all social orders and hierarchies of classes which had been consolidated by Platonic republics and Aristotelian states. There was a religious longing to transcend those class divisions that the justice of the Communes as well as of the Renaissance city had taken to be based upon reason and nature. Both Savonarola's discontent and Machiavelli's bitterness expressed the fall of a whole civilisa-

---

[17] L. Firpo, *Lo stato ideale della Controriforma*, Bari, 1957, pp. 241ff. Cp. C. Curcio, ed., *Utopisti e riformatori italiani del Cinquecento*, Bologna, 1941, and *Utopisti italiani del Cinquecento*, Rome, 1944.

tion. The fifteenth century finally revealed its ambiguity: beyond the annunciation of a regeneration, there lay the sadness of a setting sun. While the splendid cities were declining in a religious climate of expectation, people demanded a total regeneration of mankind as well as a complete change of the human condition. They were waiting for the liberation of man from the slavery to nature and her laws. No matter how different from one another, the solar city of Campanella and the New Atlantis of Francis Bacon were meant to answer these longings. In the new century there was on one side a religious reform and on the other, modern science: both were completely without nostalgia for the past.

THE UNIVERSALITY OF
LEONARDO[1]

❡ The universality of Leonardo can have many different meanings, and though all connected, they can for present purposes be distinguished from one another. Above all his universality means the width of his horizon, that is, the fact that his work and his interests had no boundaries and extended to every field of human activity and every sphere of reality. They extended to the totality of things. In this sense he once wrote that "the painter has to try to be a universal man" and that he must never sacrifice anything of the richness of Being. On the other hand, one can understand by universality something connected with value. In this sense it is not so much something all-embracing as an essential acquisition, a value connected with the wish to preserve something forever. In this second sense of universality what matters is not so much the number of the problems faced by Leonardo or the quantity of observations

---

[1] In this chapter Vasari has been used according to Milanesi, ed., *Opere*, Florence, 1906, Vol. IV, pp. 17–52. The so-called *Trattato della pittura* has been used according to the edition by Borzelli (Lanciano, Carabba, 1924).

and discoveries he happened to make. What matters is the depth of his explorations and the newness of the words, be it even one single word, he used to describe them.

If we understand the meaning of universality in this second sense, we are unfortunately faced by an almost unsurmountable difficulty. For Leonardo himself never really committed himself to anything but lived purposely all the time at the centre of a high tension. He gazed at all possible horizons of reality. At any one time he gathered the whole of reality into himself as if he were the centre and thus sought to make himself confront the meaning of human life at the point where all things meet in infinity, where the world appears a single unity in the eye and the mind of man. One might even say that here we find both the origin and the resolution of the whole enigma of Leonardo. For the enigma has something to do with the connection between his indefatigable search for the meaning of things, beings, and phenomena and his awareness that their secret root is to be found in a rationality which the human mind gathers to its own fold. On one side we have his insatiable curiosity. He is sensitive even to the most fleeting and fragile image—to the steaming mists, to the clouds which dissolve, to the moulds which form bizarre arabesques on walls. And on the other side he fixes his mind on such notions as number or absolute truth. These are indeed the two terms which we meet all the time in his writings: at one end of the scale there is experience and ever more experience; and at the other end, reason. What really matters is the manner in which these two extremes are joined to one another. Or better, the manner in which Leonardo has concretely conceived the magical point of their mingling. He certainly knew how to reveal that secret of life to us.

It is in this that Leonardo's whole significance and universal value consist. It has often been easier and more tempting to find the meaning of his work in the marvellous wealth of his researches, which covered the whole field of experience, and in the extraordinary variety of his exploratory adventures. Hence the re peated attempts to reconstruct Leonardo's universality with all its weird ideas and illusions; hence the myth of Leonardo the omniscient man, the *magus;* hence the conventional rhetorical phrases about the Leonardo who was so divine as to appear inhuman. And all the time one lost sight of the true Leonardo—of the artist who was so very human, who managed to link all knowledge and all creativity in his few great masterpieces and in hundreds of drawings. One also obscured the Leonardo who in one single insight or act or figure succeeded in conveying reality's most profound sense, that is, the relation between the appearance of the world and its transcendent secret. For Leonardo, in order to discover this relationship, had searched ceaselessly among even the most hidden aspects of things.

For this reason, Leonardo's scientific knowledge is the knowledge of the painter. His scientific knowledge forms an integral part of his art, which is the art of the painter. If we understand that science and that art, we understand the greatness and the significance of Leonardo. But his science is not that of Galileo; nor is his art that of the aesthetic theories of the twentieth century. If we see in him the precursor of theories and technical discoveries made centuries later we are precluded from understanding those unique texts in which Leonardo, fighting against himself as it were, pursued his lifelong idea that the extraordinary images he had conceived could be resolved into numbers.

"The painter's mind endeavours to be a mirror, for a mirror always makes itself have the colour of the object that is reflected by it. A mirror is indeed full of as many things as happen to stand opposite it. A painter ought to know therefore that he cannot be good at his craft unless he is a universal master of creating through his art all the qualities of the forms which nature produces. But this cannot be done unless he sees them and retraces them in his mind . . . And in fact, whatever is in the universe as essence, occurrence, or imagination, the painter must first have in his mind and then in his hands. His hands must be of such excellence that they can shape things into a well-proportioned harmony by a single glance and take no more time doing it than it takes the things to be." (Ms. A, 82r)

Here we are right at the centre of Leonardo's meditations and of his work—at the point where knowing and making coincide. He conceived the artist's work as the active synthesis of all human efforts, of science and technology, philosophy and poetry, that is, as the conclusion to every problem which might arise in connection with reality. The painter, far from being nature's slave or instrument, "debates and competes with her; he is her master and god."

Nevertheless, there stands between us and the true Leonardo, caught in the technology-science-art complex, another, more ancient image of Leonardo, an ambiguous and Faustian one. According to this image, Leonardo possessed total and secret knowledge and is supposed to have gone to the bottom of all sciences and to have foreseen all inventions. He is supposed to have known everything and to have been capable of doing everything. Not long ago a distinguished scholar (L. Heydenreich) wrote that "if one searches the enormous quantity of materials scattered over thousands of pages, and sorts them according to our orderly criterion, one gets the impression that Leonardo had in mind something like a display, in encyclopaedic form, of human knowledge in its totality. This encyclopaedia would probably have comprised the following main sections: optics, as the presupposition of all perception; mechanics, as the science of the physical forces underlying the organic as well as the inorganic natural world; biology, as the science of the laws which govern life and the development of organic matter with anatomy as the central theme; cosmology, as the science of the form of inorganic matter and of the forces which sustain these forms." One ought to add mathematics as the very premiss and the logico-methodological instrument; and morals, as the science of behaviour and as the final conclusion.

There is more: according to many scholars, Leonardo's chief merit is supposed to have been his insistence on the ever-growing autonomy of scientific research. This autonomy was to have been developed especially in regard to the arts and the training of an artist, giving them real breathing-room. It is hard to say whether this ideal view of Leonardo's omniscience owes more to medieval dreams of magic or to the conquests of modern technology. In order to assign once more a genuine meaning to Leonardo's humanity —a humanity which was neither erudition nor philology, neither mere technology nor pure art—it is necessary to follow the opposite path. One must discard the image of the ancient *magus* as well as that of the modern technician, of the scientist who dries up the artist. Only in this way can one hope to recover the true meaning of Leonardo's tension which resulted from the fact that Leonardo's original and dispassionate investigation of nature, his grand artistic creation, had yielded a completely revolutionary conception of the world. Only if one dissipates the vulgar Faustian myth can rhetorical praises as well as destructive criticism be avoided. But one can dissipate the myth fully only if one understands the reasons for its origin.

The myth of Leonardo is very old; at least in part it goes right back to his own taste for originality and detachment, halfway between irony and polemics. We can see the myth at work in Vasari, who tended to present it as factual history. Everybody knows the opening lines of Vasari's *Life:* Leonardo, "truly miraculous and heavenly," is placed, right from his birth, on a level all his own. There he was alone, tied up in a mysterious plot. "The greatest gifts are seen to have been showered by celestial influences upon human bodies, often naturally, but at times supernaturally. Beauty, gracefulness, and virtue can all be assembled in one single body in such a way that every action of such a man can be divine. Such a man leaves all other men behind and this manifestation is known for the thing it is—a gift from God, and not as something which has been acquired by human artfulness. People saw Leonardo as such a man."

It is no accident that this recital begins with astrology. It seems to go back to an observation by Leonardo himself: "There is nothing in astrology which is not a function of visual lines and perspective, i.e. astrology is the daughter of painting." Astrological constellations are the prelude to the appearance of an exceptional presence. The whole discourse emphasises throughout the exceptional nature of the man, and terms like "divine," "marvellous," and "miraculous" are used time and again. One must also emphasise the arrangement of the physical features of this portrait: extraordinary physical beauty and invincible fascination. "He was beautiful, and the splendour of his appearance cheered every sad soul." He had intellect as well as a good memory and a supreme talent for drawing. He kept nature under constant observation and was always ready to come, in tender love, to the succour of every living creature. He was extremely subtle and whimsical, without being a poseur, and still according to Vasari, all this was accompanied by a "perfect alertness, beauty, and gracefulness." His unbounded curiosity was converted miraculously into a scientific inquiry which knew no bounds and manifested itself all the time in the construction of models and plans. At the same time, the figure of the artist is presented as standing at the point of an extraordinary convergence of stellar and supernatural influxes. It is as if it were surrounded by a halo of magical power, incantation, and highly unnatural seduction. Vasari insists that when Leonardo spoke he "deprived his affirmation as well as his denial of their sharp edges." When he designed projects, he managed to win over everybody, as on the occasion when he planned to raise the whole Baptistery of Florence in order to place a grid of wooden foundations underneath without damaging the building. Everybody was persuaded that the plan was feasible; everybody, that is, "except one man—and that one man, knowing well that the idea was incapable of realisation, had taken his departure."

It was no accident that Vasari kept repeating such tales. He wanted to point to the air of mysteriousness that had hung about Leonardo's speculations on nature, and to re-create the mist that had enveloped him and had made him appear at the same time astonished and horrified. Hence he lingers in his description of the room where only the artist had been allowed to enter, for it was a room populated by "reptiles, lizards, crickets, snakes, butterflies, locusts, moths, and other weird species of similar animals." By contrast, there is mention of Leonardo's love of birds: "Often, when walking through the places where they sell birds, he would take them from the cage by hand and, having paid the price demanded by the vendor, he let them fly into the air, giving them back the liberty they had lost." And this was the same man who had dissected and explored the bodies of beasts and men, and had talked freely about the disgusting smell he had to overcome and about the awful sight of putrefying flesh. And then there was the sheer extravagance of his own life: "One might say that he owned nothing. He worked very little, but all the time kept servants and horses." If one analyses Vasari's pages minutely and with

patience one will find again and again, through the
repetition of certain words, that Vasari's main concern
was to evoke a strange and ambiguous figure that was
not human. He intended it perhaps to be divine;
certainly bordering on the demonic. For in that particular part of the fifteenth century, a natural philosopher who intended to break with the traditions of
the closed schools in order to re-establish a direct
contact with the bodily reality of things, and wrest
from them the secret hidden behind their appearances,
could not be anything but demonic. "He shaped in
his mind some very subtle and marvellously fine
points which he could never have expressed with his
hands, no matter how excellent. And his intellectual
caprices were such that in philosophising about natural things he was led to an understanding of the
properties of herbs and to the observation of the
movements of the heavenly spheres, the course of
the moon and the paths of the sun." In the first edition
of his *Lives*, Vasari had significantly added: "For this
reason he fashioned in his soul a concept so heretical
that it was alien to any religion whatever, and thus
he turned out to be much more of a philosopher than
a Christian." This is not the place to investigate
whether Leonardo was a believer. Here we are only
interested in emphasising the many different features
of his personality. There was his elegant and hand-
some appearance and his unique hair style, and the
fact that, without means, he kept horses and servants.
Absorbed in his idiosyncratic thoughts and his private
dreams, he was both gentle and enigmatic and frequently given to meditation rather than to work, intent upon spying on the mysteries of nature among
strange and repulsive beasts. And yet, he did it with
a truly Franciscan gesture of love towards birds, his
eyes turned towards the playfulness of clouds, colours, and shadows. Captivated by projects that were
incapable of realisation, he never finished his own
works. But when by chance he did finish them, they

turned out to be living creatures. There is an ambiguity here, full of meaningful allusions: on one hand, there was his restlessness which could not be alleviated and which forced him to abandon many a work because he was always pursued by the infinite number of possible forms which faced him every time he attempted a definition and a fixed shape. And on the other hand he veritably managed to infuse life into his creations—a life which his highly contrived artfulness seemed to be able to achieve in plain competition with nature: "With good rules, better order, correct measurement . . . he truly gave to his figures both motion and breath." At this point one really ought to ask oneself whether Vasari knew of the theories which had been fashionable among the Neoplatonists half a century earlier, theories about theurgic practices concerned with the possibility of attracting living spirits to graven images by ensuring the complete perfection of the work of art.

However this may be, Vasari succeeded singularly well in his purpose. He left Leonardo's quest for the totality of reality, no matter how trivial and how humble the reality, completely out of account. Thus he was left with airy designs, and with architectural marvels, rather than with those projects which had led Leonardo into the sewers of Milan and the brothels of Pavia. And thus he was clearly left with the task of placing Leonardo somewhere between the divine and the satanic, between science and magic, between the animating power of art and the necromantic evocation of dark powers. The well-known difference between the first and the second edition of the *Life* documents not so much the heresy and the final repentance of our artist as the method of the biographer who, having allowed himself a full fling in conjuring up a Faustian image of his hero, felt obliged, after a certain amount of time had passed, to tone everything down. The original passages about Leonardo's lack of piety were suppressed in the later version. They had not really been truthful but had followed, by some kind of rhetorical necessity, from the general portrait Vasari had initially had in mind. But whether dictated by historical truthfulness or not they had imposed themselves upon Vasari by a sort of internal consistency with the whole image he had fashioned. At the turning point of the century a person like the one envisaged by Vasari could not but be something of a rebel in religious matters. It was, so to speak, a matter of style.

Now that we have become aware of these peculiarities of Vasari's we may run through the text of the *Life* again from the beginning. We will then find that none of the ingredients necessary for a portrait of the magician is missing. There is the stellar conjunction, the convergence of astral influxes, and there is astrology. On the other side, there is the empirical investigation of nature, the experiments, mathematical reason, the herbs, and unclean animals such as serpents and bats. Then there are the tinctures and all the characteristic products of hermetic and alchemical science. And finally there are the theurgic practices and the power to give real life to pictures. Nothing is missing, not even the repentance before death. The first edition of Vasari's *Life* contained also the following passage, which was suppressed later: "In the end, having become old, he was ill for many months. And when he saw himself near death he kept talking of religious matters and returned to the good path and, with many tears, embraced the faith." In the second edition we read: "Seeing himself near death he was desirous of learning about matters Catholic and of our good and sacred Christian religion." In this second edition the philosopher of nature and the consciously rebellious magician is replaced by nothing more lively than a man who happens to be somewhat unconversant with the religion of his ancestors.

This, then, is Vasari's story. It is transparent in its

intentions, made to a certain measure and faithful no doubt to a very definite conception. The final passage which follows upon the narrative of Leonardo's death in the arms of the King of France, written no more than a few decades after the demise of the artist, amounts to one more vigorous summary of the impression present in the whole of the work, that of stupefied wonder: "Every sad soul was comforted by the splendour of his countenance, and by his words he was able to sway men's minds in any direction. His own physical strength amounted to a veritable fury and with his right hand he was able to bend the clapper of a bell and a horse-shoe as if they were made of mere lead. With his generosity he won and warmed the hearts of all his friends, rich as well as poor, as long as they had intellect and talent. His mere presence honoured and decorated every room, no matter how wretched and deplete." This is an epitaph—but one charged with allusions, no matter how trite, of great symbolic significance. This is true for the king's embrace as well as for Leonardo's power to redeem things that are vile, for his ability to gladden people's hearts as well as his physical power, for his dress as well as his comportment.

It has been necessary to dwell at length on Vasari's portrait in order to show how far back the origins of that image, which is in a sense a link between us and the historical Leonardo, go. But when we come to ask how this famous portrait ever emerged in the first place, it is not too difficult to see that in many ways Vasari made himself the faithful interpreter of what Leonardo himself had said. One might say that Vasari's major limitation is that he accepted too readily what had been suggested by both Leonardo himself and some contemporary observers. Thus there came to be reflected in Vasari's portrait the outlines of Leonardo's self-portrait, intentionally designed for purposes both polemical and ironical. If we want, today, to understand Leonardo we must above all

understand the meaning of his irony and his polemical
attitudes without becoming captive to either. Leonardo displayed contempt of as well as humility
towards the learned world, replete with the most over-
refined forms of culture. This is where we must take
our beginning.

The artist is a craftsman. He is not a man of pure
culture, but a mechanic. He confronts the learned
men of the schools as well as the civilised courtiers
who teach the sciences in the universities and cultivate
literature in the liberal circles which had formed
around both the old and the new princes. In the
course of the fifteenth and sixteenth centuries the
impact of the arts tended to undermine the traditional scheme of things. Technology, both in architecture and in engineering, became more and more
refined and thus tended to destroy the old barriers
between mathematics and the practical, mechanical
sciences. In unforgettable pages Vespasiano da Bisticci
tells us that Brunelleschi, without any literary education, was said to have gone to the school of the
learned Toscanelli and to have developed quite suddenly from pupil to master. All the same, it is not
true that the relationship between the arts and the
sciences was completely reversed in a short span.
Painters, sculptors, and architects were not immediately accorded the dignity of scientists. In the case
of Leonardo, who knew very little Latin and no Greek
and had only the slightest knowledge of religious matters and then only by hearsay, this reversal took the
form of a constant rebellion. He was not only aware
of the sterility of the medieval schools but also sensed
the vacuousness of humanistic learning. He launched
his protest in the name of a new type of man, another
form of science and culture, another mode of understanding the tasks and functions of mankind. Thus
he remained consciously separated from the "company of men alien to his studies," kept aloof from

other people's cares, and was wholly absorbed in his mathematical contemplations.

We can discern in his rebellion and criticism, articulate as well as inarticulate, a variety of aspects and themes. We must try to distinguish between those of his attitudes which were tied up with a particular historical situation and those which belong to the eternally valid profile of the discoverer, the scientist, and the artist. And above all, we must always bear in mind the proud humility of the craftsman who is always moving through "the poor towns" with his humble merchandise. Leonardo was all the time fighting against vain words, empty speeches, and abstract arguments, against books full of wind, against the pseudo-sciences, the pseudo-philosophies, and the screaming noise of public debates forever incapable of reaching the peaceful silence of well-established conclusions. He fought through his senses, his experience, his hands, his works, his engines, and his craft. "It is truly so that wherever there is a lack of reason, there is a surfeit of shouting. This never happens when one is preoccupied with matters that are certain. We say therefore that where there is shouting there is no science, for the truth has only one goal: when it is made public there is an end to the dispute. And if there ever is a new argument about it, it is one arising from lies and a confusion of facts and is not a renewal of a genuine quest."

There was in Leonardo an open defiance of that whole world which had, in some way, made words the centre of all arguments, disputes, and researches. In that world the victory never went to experimental proof or to mathematics, but to the master of dialectics. "The true knowledge is the knowledge which experience has caused to enter through the senses and which has thereby silenced verbal arguments. It is a knowledge which does not nourish its upholders by dreams but by first and true principles. It proceeds by sure and progressive steps to the goal, as can be demonstrated in the principles of mathematics, that is, those of numbering and measuring, known as arithmetics and geometry. These latter sciences deal with the utmost truth of both continuous and discontinuous quantity. Here there is no argument whether two threes make more or less than six or whether in a triangle the sum of the angles is less than two right angles. Every type of argument will be destroyed by eternal silence and brought to a peaceful conclusion. For this is something the mendacious mental sciences cannot do." (*Trattato di pittura*, 29)

Leonardo added another protest to his protest against the mental sciences, against philosophising in terms of grand questions—such as those which concerned themselves with the essence of God and the soul—which were always disputed by the various upholders of contradictory verbal expressions. He also protested against contemplative knowledge which refused to dirty its hands and combine thought with works. Such knowledge never verified concepts by looking at things and observing the changes which work wrought upon them. He shouted at his imaginary opponent: "If you say that these true and well-known sciences are part of mechanics because they can never be brought to fruition except by the work of hands, . . . then it seems to me that all those sciences which are not derived from experience are vain and full of errors. For experience is the mother of all certainty. The sciences which do not have their end, middle, and beginning in the experience which comes through the five senses are useless." The mind is the mediator. It is an admirable instrument provided it is accompanied by eyes and hands, and leads from bodily reality, with the help of mathematics, to a new reality transfigured by man's hands. But if one isolates and separates thought from one's senses, one pretends to be debating with God in solitary contemplation, and in this way the mind remains sterile and is nourished by nothing but words, i.e. by endless noise.

All in all—and this is important—Leonardo not only renewed the scientific method, but he also stood on its head the relationship between man and the world. He changed the whole conception of reality. At the end of the fifteenth century and the dawn of the sixteenth, the praise of man's dignity was a commonplace, and it was widely held that the whole universe was gathered in the mind, the centre of being. Some had even gone further and had written pages of dazzling eloquence to prove that man was divine because he was the free creator of his own self, independent of natural causes. For man's nature, they had argued, is the fruit of his actions. Leonardo went even further. But he never contented himself with a general affirmation. In this refusal thus to content himself he gave a final definition of the meaning of human action as well as of the character of his whole work. Man in the last analysis does not realise himself through spiritual or moral activity. By themselves, spiritual and mental actions are sterile and useless. A worthwhile act must originate in the senses and, in the end, have a repercussion on the senses. The circle which Leonardo was thinking of is the circle which extends from the eye (i.e. from a profound vision into reality, into the darkest of cavities) to the mind and returns to things through the activity of the hands or through some other kind of bodily movement. This last move completes the circuit. The symbol of this circuit is to be found in the painter, whose eye is the knowledge, the most subtle kind of knowledge, which pursues, well below the surface appearances of things, all original forces to their very roots. From there the eye ascends again to numbers and reason in order to end up designing forms which are not just the surfaces of things, a sort of skin, but the immanent force of things; thus the secret of the world is made manifest in an image which comprehends the whole of reality. Leonardo's few pictures, therefore, represent a veil; but at the same time they also unveil the whole of Being.

But before we discuss the science which to Leonardo is the only true science, that of the painter, it is necessary to emphasise his proud defence of mechanics, of the manual crafts, in which, as in mathematics, he saw the triumph of human dignity. Petrarch, in texts which have rightly become famous, had considered it a mark of inferiority that certain disciplines had to make use of manual work, and to come into contact with bodies and manual operations. But Leonardo gave a new and very concrete sense to the value of man in his open and outspoken declaration that man's value consists in his ability to transform a work into a concept. Such a concept, to be functional, has to link itself to things even as it emerges from them. Man has a value and a central significance because he performs in the world a conscious and active function, because he discovers the forces operative in the world, and through the mediation of mathematics, which is both order and harmony, gives them a new shape in a superior harmony. Such reshaping, however, can only be fruitful and meaningful if it does not consist in and is not exhausted in words or mental images. It must not be a mere concept or thought. It must be a thing, a body, a machine, and must take its place in universal nature. Neither eyes nor minds, neither the mental sciences nor the visual sciences, suffice: in every case there must be manual operations.

There is no need to quote any of Leonardo's many passages on this subject. But it is useful to watch his attack, often implicit, on a culture which consisted of books, quotations, recitals, and summaries of past knowledge, in this light. Leonardo denied neither the importance of history and antiquity nor the faculty of memory which enables us to perceive the "passage of time." But he did attack authority when opposed to experience, the notion of culture as a passive acceptance, and the idea that knowledge is not invention but mere conservation.

In the *Atlantic Codex* the same subject is discussed in an even more lapidary and incisive manner. There we find it as a general premise and as a motto to his whole work. "I know only too well that since I am not a man of letters, someone who is presumptuous could with some reason criticise me by alleging that I am a man without education. Foolish people! . . . They will say that I, because I have no literary education, am not competent to speak of the things I am speaking of. These people do not know that the things I am speaking about are things to be dealt with by experience rather than by other people's words. Experience was the task-master of those who first wrote about it; and I too will take it to be my task-master and in all cases I will obey it" (119v. a). Leonardo, therefore, never quoted authors but always experience, "the master of their masters." The experimenter—and this is important—is always an inventor. Leonardo contrasted activity and works to passivity, reception, and conservation. Unfortunately the words he employed were ambiguous and open to a variety of interpretations. Take "experience": conventionally experience means collection, reception, cataloguing; whereas for Leonardo it meant work, invention, activity, and labour. "These people become blustering and pompous, dressed and adorned not in their own, but in other people's labours. And these same people are unwilling to give me credit for my labours. If they despise my inventions, they are even more contemptible because they are not even inventors, but only trumpets and records of other people's inventions; and as such they are much to be criticised" (*Cod. Atl.* 117r, b). In this sense all experimentation, since it is a mediation between nature as it actually is and the realization of all the possibilities, is on one hand an understanding of real and necessary processes, and on the other a constructive labour. Hence the condemnation of people who are mere trumpets, of the alchemists whose experimentation is purely accidental, casual, and arbitrary. Leonardo issued a solemn warning to people who want to make gold. If you want to make gold, he said, go into the mines and surprise nature as she is making the gold and then make use of the forces and numbers you have thus discovered. This advice brings out very clearly what Leonardo meant when he spoke of man as a mediator between the artifices of nature and the new world of human products.

Or take the word "mirror": here again is an image capable of many variations and full of the rich ambiguity of a great many meanings. If one could follow all the oscillations of this word and of the implied figures of speech, one could perhaps penetrate further into the mind of Leonardo. The mind of the painter is supposed to be a mirror. But the people who recite and who act as trumpets are also mirrors. On one side "mirror" means something like an active gathering of the infinite "species" of the world; on the other side it means the annihilation of the mind vis-à-vis the thinness of the object and, above all, the passivity of pure receptiveness as contrasted to the activity of the inventor who serves as interpreter between nature and man. In both senses, the dominant preoccupation is revealed. Knowledge is an activity, an activity intrinsic to the functioning of the mind, designed to become manifest and extrinsic in the work produced. The drawings which play such an important part in Leonardo's manuscripts afford us many precious insights. In these drawings Leonardo himself tells us that in doing them the manual operation becomes explicit and the purely mental apperception is overcome. And what is more it is overcome in a more effective way than by the written word. Leonardo sought to explain this conception, difficult even for him, on a variety of levels and, by way of example, used to say that a man in love will always prefer the painter's picture of his beloved to a writer's description of her. In another place he argued that while the mental image and the spoken word "remain in the mind of their author," the drawing provides something concrete, "that is, an operation much more worthy than the above-mentioned contemplation or knowledge."

If one wishes to go further and risk formulating something like a general theory, no matter how hypothetical, one might say this. In Leonardo's conception of experience, a drawing is an absolutely necessary ingredient of knowledge and as such plays an even greater importance than it does as a mere instrument of expression. The relationship between drawings and thoughts in Leonardo's manuscripts has never been studied properly. But one can see nevertheless that Leonardo proceeded towards a whole anatomy of reality through his drawings and thus used them to make all sense experiences more profound and to reduce every phenomenon to its structure—a structure which in the last analysis is always a mechanico-mathematical structure. When Leonardo, in his notes, reduced the functioning of an animal organism to its components and then traced it back to a play of forces between "mechanical instruments," his eyes always gradually cut through the various levels in which reality makes itself explicit. He went through them, turned them into a scheme and rendered all their separate elements manifest. On one side there are his drawings; on the other his theoretical reflections. They all point to a unitary vision of things in their innermost structure, reducible to a model which is a machine or a play of forces and movements. And this is true even for life in all its manifestations. In his *Anatomical Notebooks* of the Windsor Library we can read as follows: "Nature cannot give movement to animals without mechanical instruments. This much is proved, to my mind, by

the native forces created by nature herself in animals."
The idea of a machine, a machine which can be
taken to pieces, comes out more and more frequently
in his reflections on anatomy written after 1500: "If
you speculate about this our (human) machine, do
not be saddened by the thought that your knowledge
depends on someone else's death; but rejoice at the
fact that our creator on high has fashioned our intellect that it can be an excellent instrument for such
perception." A few pages above he shows himself
wholly absorbed in a description of the functioning
of the animal machine: "The same happens in the
bodies of the animals. The beating of the heart gen-
erates a wave of blood which passes through all the
veins which continuously are dilated and constrict
themselves. The dilation comes from receiving the
blood, and the constriction from letting the super-
abundance of blood go out. This teaches us the beating of the pulse." Man is a machine; the animals are
machines ("Man does not differ from the animals
except in accidentals"); the whole world is a machine.
The spirits are the motor power of these machines.
Or, perhaps better, the spirit is a drive or force,
understood as something incorporeal but physical,
something surrounded by a penumbra of ambiguity.
"So far we have said that the definition of the spirit is
a power joined to the body, because it cannot move
itself by itself . . . for if the spirit is an incorporeal
quantity, such quantity would have to be said to be
vacuous; but this cannot be for nature does not have
a vacuum."

Machines and instruments, forces and matter: Leonardo's anatomy, which is developed step by step
through optics, general mechanics, and a physical
interpretation of the universe, finally reveals an inter-
play of canals, flow and counter-flow, cords, levers,
weights, primary and secondary motors, and is full
of forces which are being transferred and modified.
Facing the soul, Leonardo's thoughts grind to a halt.

Having demonstrated the soul's physical components he came to that final conclusion, ironical to some and terribly serious to others: "The remainder of the definition of the soul I will leave in the minds of the monks, the fathers of the people, who by inspiration know all the secrets."

This is not the place to pursue this topic. It is of greater importance to discuss how the study of anatomy gradually reveals reality to the eye and the hand of the painter. For it is here, at the very limits of scientific anatomy, that one witnesses a double conversion. On one side the study of anatomy is turned into a technology which invents new machines; and on the other it is transformed into painting. We are always, and this is worth stressing, within the realm of the highest of the sciences, the science which embraces all the others including philosophy, that is, within the realm of the science of painting. The painter must fathom the very bottom of reality and define and describe all the elements and forces and their functioning. When he has reached the innermost ground and discovered the secret of the world's natural machine, he can proceed to the construction of artificial machines. Reality is like a "threatening and dark cave." Leonardo faced that cave, not only "eager to see the great multitude of different and strange forms made by the artfulness of nature" but also to learn to reproduce these forms as machines.

Among all the machines invented by Leonardo his flying machine has always been the one to appeal most to the imagination of mankind. If one traces his thoughts, his observations, and his plans on this matter, one will understand very clearly the double process of which we have spoken. There is first the discovery of the bird as a natural machine. Then there is the human construction of the artificial bird. One ought to consult the famous passage in the *Atlantic Codex:* "The bird is an instrument operating through mathematical laws. This instrument is in the power of the man who can create it with his own movements. But he lacks the actual power of the bird . . . Thus we might say that this instrument, made by man, is lacking in nothing except the soul of the bird. This soul has to be imitated, like a counterfeit, by the soul of man." Soul, in this sense, Leonardo explains, is nothing but the force of propulsion.

The whole marvellous range of Leonardo's universal science is displayed in the chapters of a treatise about the anatomy of the universe, in which the mechanism of its functioning is discovered, dissected, and translated into drawings and plans. From this analysis Leonardo proceeds to composition. And from these inventions, in competition with nature as it were, but always obedient to her exigencies and her rationality, there arise the machines. Studies of physics and technical elaborations run parallel with drawings, and they are based upon his unitary conception of the world, one which includes the phenomena of life and which is formulated in terms of mechanical principles capable of mathematical expression.

There is a famous text by Vitruvius who was loved as well as hated by the great men of the fifteenth century (Ghiberti quoted him; but Alberti despised him). Vitruvius had written that an architect has to know everything and must be something like a walking encyclopaedia. He has to be a man of letters so that he can fill in gaps when writing from memory. He has to be able to draw in order to make plans. He has to know geometry and arithmetic to be able to calculate. He has to know optics to study the light, and so on. But Leonardo's universal science—and we must never forget this—is painting. And it is universal not because it contains a bit of everything, but because through it the eternal shapes of the real world are expressed in the way in which they really are and not as they appear on the surface. The supreme manifestation thus revealed is the innermost being. And this science thus penetrates to the innermost roots of things, cutting through all structures and levels. "If you despise a painting which is only an imitation of the works evident in nature, you will despise for certain a subtle invention which, with the help of minute and philosophical speculation, reflects the quality of shapes. Oceans, sites, plants, animals, herbs, flowers—they are all surrounded by lights and shadows. A painting is the true and legitimate daughter of nature; for painting is indeed born from nature herself."

It is not enough to know a little of everything. The eye of the painter, which must take in the whole of reality and not only the appearances, must descend to the very bottom of the dark cave and discover in all its structures and operations the machine that the world is—the flow and counter-flow of blood in living beings, and of water in the rivers and oceans of the vast body of the earth. In the end, his vision must penetrate further, through all the various forces which agitate the world. And then the hands of the great recorder must make drawings of everything, and from these drawings, reconstruct the machines in competition with nature. Leonardo's drawings and machines correspond to his studies of physics and anatomy and are the technico-scientific aspects of his initiation. The final accomplishment, however, lies elsewhere. The whole of his physics is a presupposition, something merely preliminary, to that which is the genuinely metaphysical aspect of his work, those few paintings in which he rises to a vision which no longer sees instruments and machines as components of reality, but rather reality itself in all its totality and perfection. Without the analysis, the synthesis would not have been possible. Yet the synthesis infinitely surpasses the sum total of the elements of the analysis.

For this reason we have so many of his drawings, notes, and sketches for books, and so very few paintings. Leonardo knew, more or less consciously, that the last word is one only, that in a single face or a single landscape, everything else is condensed. But he also knew that that final and total vision is not given except to him who penetrates to the very ground of the mystery of being.

It would be easy to list the texts Leonardo has written about this voyage of discovery and this analysis of every region of experience, an analysis which is made to converge in the consciousness of mankind, and of which the works of men are the precipitate. Science amounts to the penetration of reality in all directions. It comprises all techniques, i.e. the artificial reproduction of everything which exists, so that the synthesis, or the meaning, can be re-established in a form.

Leonardo was an outsider. He even took a certain pleasure in the fact that he was surrounded by an aura of magic and by bizarre mysteries. Among all the men of his century he insisted with the greatest clarity on the relationship between the infinite multiplicity of processes and the point at which they reduce themselves to a meaning: this, to him, was the revelation of a mystery which in spite of the revelation remained a mystery. He had no doubt that the secrets of the cave were reducible to numbers, forces, weights and levers, pulls and pushes. But although the face of his Virgin is the complex of these numbers and elements and is not without the flow and counterflow of the blood in the flesh, it is at the same time infinitely more than the sum total of these elements and movements. Leonardo has told us as nobody else has done that the reality which the painter must portray is the vortex of elements and their numbers, a whirlpool of forces and yet also the harmonious composition of these forces. For this reason he has presented us with an image of reality on the level of chaos, and as a counterpoint, its formal resolution. It is for this reason that all his shapes are informed by everything that is chaotic in the nether world. Though utterly naturalistic, they show at the same time everything which is below as well as everything which is above the world of our experience. They truly grasp the whole of consciousness.

In order to paint a face, or better, the meaning of a face—its reality and truth—it is necessary to have knowledge of all the muscles under the skin, of all the vessels and organs in their most minute details. One has to know the bones and watch the putrefaction of a body and notice the stench. One has to have watched the changing expressions of the emotions, the changes wrought by lights and shadows and the ways in which faces become old and fade. And one has to know the laws of and the reasons for all these processes.

There is no reason why we should allow Leonardo to deceive us. His irony made him fond of presenting a very ambiguous picture of himself. But we can today easily free ourselves from that picture and see through it. He derided magicians, necromancers, and alchemists. But he found it amusing to make people wonder whether he himself was not to be found by any chance among them. People also thought of him as a scientist because he searched at the bottom of the dark cave for the ultimate ground of things, because he investigated the laws of the motion of the earth, of water and of light. They also considered him an engineer because of his interest in machines and instruments. And his linguistic dexterity made him into something of a writer, or even poet. But only he who understands the meaning of the science of painting will understand Leonardo's search for the point at which eye and hand meet; at which historical analysis, practical action, and artistic expression meet as the full comprehension of totality.

In those same years Michelangelo managed to express in stone the meaning of an infinite tragedy and to harmonise it with a peaceful composition. When one peruses the descriptions of cataclysmic tempests and deluges which occupied the last years of Leonardo's life and if one thinks of his terrifying and thunderous images of the dying world, one is forced to think of Savonarola and Michelangelo. In Leonardo the mystery of the Apocalypse became more and more evident and during his last years he became obsessed by it. The very forces whose power he had investigated seemed to explode and the whole man seemed to be overwhelmed by this cosmic explosion. Visions of the death of man, indeed of the whole death of being and of submersion into nothingness, followed one upon another, one more terrifying and gigantic than the other. The irony of a universe without measure and limit that had suggested certain strange images of Gulliver-like titans, now led to complete terror. The tension created by the ascent from chaos to form became too great. It burst and chaos re-emerged. The forests died and the mountains broke open. The wind and the sea, "the air covered by dark clouds and pierced by serpent-like motions of infuriated heavenly arrows, were illuminated here and there in the darkness of the night."

With these words Leonardo expressed in obsessive images his dark foreboding of the fall of an ancient world, of a human society in decline, and of an order that was disappearing. The passage quoted is from the manuscript preserved in the library of Windsor Castle. But in these same pages he also has another message, an invitation to respect the miraculous works of nature. It is something wicked, he says, to destroy them, "and the greatest wickedness of all is to take life away from a man." "One must not wish that one's ire and evil temper destroy that life . . . which parts most unwillingly from this body, and I certainly believe that its wailing and pain is not without reason."

Here we find Leonardo's authentic magic, his full sensation, positive and carnal, of reality; and also his painful awareness of all human limitations. All this is very human and therefore universal.

GALILEO
AND THE CULTURE OF HIS AGE

❡ Between 1924 and 1928 Benedetto Croce wrote a series of essays in *La Critica*. They have become very well known and have since been collected in his *Storia dell'età barocca in Italia*. They dealt with what he described as those "great spiritual movements, so specifically Italian," the Renaissance and the Counter-reformation, and in an attempt to clarify the concept of the Baroque, Croce defined Italian "decadence." "There was a decadence of moral enthusiasm, a decadence of common ardour and of research, of the anxieties, the joys, and the labours of indefatigable activity." Nevertheless he discovered even in that uniform grey some "lively points" in Italian history. And among those the most lively was the work of Galileo. He stressed not only the importance of Galileo's scientific discoveries but the significance of his philosophy—and by philosophy he meant philosophy in the proper sense, a critical awareness of a method of research and its logical defence. He wrote that Galileo had been "a genuine philosopher in so far as he was preoccupied with methodology."[1] Galileo had objected to the old systematic

---

[1] B. Croce, *Storia dell'età barocca in Italia*, Bari, 1946, p. 62. One ought to reread Croce's whole argument, based to a large

Peripateticism, which still reigned supreme in the universities, and had opposed to it the new results of physical research, of new mathematical speculations and the new logic of the sciences.

Though unexceptionable as a whole, Croce's judgment is today in need of being made more precise. This is true not so much, as many seem to think, because we have formed a different view of Galileo's work as seen against the background of the philosophical currents of the sixteenth century; nor is it because we have now discovered that Galileo was more indebted to the mechanical arts and the technology of his age than to any grand conceptions of reality. For that matter, we do not intend to discuss, except in passing, Croce's concept of Italian decadence. We know today about the wealth of Venice, the vitality of Padua and the solidity of the Grand Duchy of Tuscany towards the end of the sixteenth century. We will let this pass. What we have to do when rereading Croce's eloquent pages is to liberate ourselves from a conception of history which is solely concerned with great periods and hence with great units of measurement such as the Renaissance, the Reformation, the Counter-reformation, and the Baroque. In such a conception of history the preoccupa-

---

extent on G. Gentile's theory as expressed in his introduction and his commentary on his selection of Galilean texts, G. Galilei, *Frammenti e lettere*, Livorno, 1917. Croce was also thinking of a work by B. Spaventa, *Un luogo di Galileo*, 1882, published by Gentile, *Scritti filosofici di B. Spaventa*, Naples, 1900, pp. 383–87, in which Galileo's theories about the relationship between human and divine knowledge are examined. One ought to remember that Croce in his presentation of Galileo's thought was still preoccupied with his attacks on positivism and with the problem of how scientific philosophy is possible. On the other hand he mistook Galileo's position on the relationship between faith and science and did not draw an adequate distinction between it and the so-called Averroistic doctrine of double truth.

tion with holistic notions, with notions of continuity, and with the permanence of certain dominant traits has crowded out all particular facts and all sensitivity to changing events—so much so that in the end the individual characteristics of a man and of his works, of institutions and events, are replaced by the dialectical play of mere categories. In this connection one is reminded of the touching falsification of the date of Galileo's birth by Vincenzio Viviani. Viviani wanted to make Galileo's birth coincide with the death of Michelangelo. So famous a scholar as Emil Wohlwill was deeply scandalised by this attempt and thought it sufficient reason to doubt everything Viviani had reported. In this he went too far, as was shown in a perhaps somewhat too passionate criticism by Antonio Favaro.[2]

In his own quiet way, Viviani only wanted to give a mythical cloak to the continuity theory of the Renaissance, that is, to the view that the spirit of rebirth and of the resurrection of antiquity had passed from the field of the arts to the field of scientific research.

As a matter of fact, the truth is that Galileo was indeed born in the year in which Michelangelo died. But on the whole, the circumstances were such as to

---

[2] On the date of Galileo's birth as treated in *Racconto istorico* by V. Viviani, and about the variations in the codices and the printed editions, see the National Edition, (hereafter cited as *Opere*], XIX, p. 599. E. Wohlwill, as is known, often and, finally, in his great work *Galilei und sein Kampf für die coppernicanische Lehre,* Hamburg and Leipzig, 1909, p. 642, attacked the credibility of the biographer Viviani. He was contradicted vigorously by A. Favaro who discussed the matter several times, in two articles in 1915 and 1916, in the *Archivio storico italiano,* as well as in his monograph on Viviani, "Amici e correspondenti di Galileo, XXIX, Vincenzio Viviani," *Atti del reale istituto veneto,* 72, pt. II, 1912, pp. 100–1. On the whole question see R. Giacomelli, *Galileo Galilei giovane e il suo 'de motu,'* Pisa, 1949, pp. 2–5.

remind us rather of the fact that he was born the year after the conclusion of the Council of Trent. For it was then that censorship began to block the circulation of ideas, seeking to protect with the utmost rigour the orthodoxy of Italy from even the slightest tremour of speculation. There is a vast distance between the early years of Michelangelo at the court of Lorenzo the Magnificent, in touch with men like Poliziano and eventually under the spell of the sermons and the martyrdom of Savonarola, and the last years of Galileo's life, during which Europe was drenched in blood by the Thirty Years' War. During that century and a half everything had changed completely. The centre of gravity of civilisation had been shifted and transformed. Instead of continuity, one gains the impression of a complete break. On August 5, 1632, Thomas Campanella wrote to Galileo from Rome: "This news of ancient truths, of new worlds, new stars, new systems, new nations, etc., is the beginning of a new age."[3] The only point is that the new age announced by Campanella is something very different from the one that had been announced, almost a century and a half before, by the followers of Savonarola. Campanella's new age is that of Bacon and Descartes, of Hobbes and Grotius, Comenius, Gassendi, Mersenne, Kepler. It is the age of Newton's

---

[3] Galileo, *Opere*, XIV, p. 367 (T. Campanella, *Lettere*, V. Spampanato, ed., Bari, 1927, p. 241). Campanella's observation on the character of the doctrines of the *Dialogo* are interesting: "they were the doctrines of the ancient Pythagoreans and Democritans." One should note also another letter by Campanella to Galileo, March 8, 1614, from Naples: "You ought to take up the perfection of mathematics and leave the atoms for later . . . and you ought to write first of all that this philosophy comes from Italy, from Filolao and Timeo in parts, and that Copernicus stole it from them." *Lettere*, p. 177; *Opere*, XII, p. 32. In *Metaphysica*, Paris, 1638, p. 216 (but here the reproduction was used, Turin, 1961), Campanella makes Galileo a follower of both Democritus and Archimedes.

Principia and Spinoza's *Ethica* as well as that of Leibniz, a new age populated by people among whom Galileo was to find his rightful place and one which would be completely incomprehensible without him. If we want to understand his work and tho role he played, there is no need for general reflections about the Renaissance and the age of the Baroque. What we need instead is a precise description of the conditions prevalent in the Italy of the last quarter of the sixteenth century. Croce thought in terms of decadence, and meant something like a fall, not only in the economic and political sense, but also in a moral and human one. Croce's reflections lose their force when one considers the achievements of Cosimo I in Tuscany, and a little later the work of Ferdinand I, or the wealth and luxury displayed in Venice during the whole of the sixteenth century and the increase in the export of woollen cloth right down to the year 1610.[4] It is not difficult to find in the ethico-political field, especially in the Republic of Venice, events that correspond to what has rightly been called "the Indian summer of the Italian economy," 1550–1620. The city that won the battle of Lepanto and managed to defend the rights of the state against papal pretensions had a governing class which certainly possessed extraordinary human quali-

---

[4] Cp. L. Bulferetti, "Galileo e la cultura del suo tempo," in *Fortuna di Galileo*, Bari, 1964, pp. 127–61, and the same author's *Galileo Galilei nella società del suo tempo*, Manduria, 1964. Cp. also the essays by Beloch, Beltrami, Silva, and Cipolla in: C. M. Cipolla, ed., *Storia dell'economia italiana*, I, Turin, 1959, esp. pp. 17–21, by Cipolla. See also A. Tenenti, *Cristoforo Da Canal. La Marine Vénitienne avant Lépant*, Paris, 1962; G. Cozzi, *Il Doge Niccolò Contarini*, Venice-Rome, 1958, and the same author's "Il *De perfectione rerum* di Niccolò Contarini," *Bollettino dell'istituto di storia della società e dello stato veneziano*, I, 1959, pp. 155–56, and my complementary note, *Giornale critico della filosofia italiana*, XL, 1961, pp. 134–36. Cp. also F. Seneca, *Il doge Leonardo Donà*, Padua, 1959.

ties. Men like the Doge Leonardo Donà and to a lesser
extent like the Doge Niccolò Contarini were of un-
usual stature. And they were by no means exceptions.
"In the Venice of the second half of the sixteenth
century there existed a class of cultivated noblemen,
solicitous for the interests of their country but also
open to the whole world, intent upon listening to its
advice and benefiting from its experience. Though
tied to the religious and cultural tradition, they were
determined to be unruffled and, informed by their
achievements and their freedom, to provide their
own answers to the many problems which the age
presented to their minds and hearts." These men had
enjoyed a philosophical education in Padua, albeit
outside the framework of official courses, and at times
even in opposition to them. They were men who promoted and countenanced the activities of Sarpi and
sought an independent political line designed to keep a
fine balance between France and Spain. With the as-
cetic austerity of their habits and their intransigent
fidelity to the teachings of Christ, they found the
strength to oppose the undue pretensions of the church
in the temporal field as well as in the realm of ideas. A
foreign resident in Venice reported that no less a
person than a Donà, during an altercation about
prohibited books, had "dismissed (an inquisitor) with
insulting words." He had, in fact, spat in his face and
"booksellers were given permission to sell their books,
no matter whether prohibited or not. Only if they
paid for these books could the inquisitors burn them
as they liked, like any commodity one has bought;
but not otherwise."[5]

Fulganzio Micanzio, a faithful friend of Galileo,
recalled with moving words in his biography of Sarpi
(who admired Galileo without reservation) "the civil

---

[5] For this and other documents cited see A. Rotondò,
"Nuovi documenti per la storia dell'Indice dei libri proibiti,
1572–1638," *Rinascimento*, N.S. III, 1963, pp. 145–211.

and liberal manner" in which the meetings at the resort of the Morosini had been conducted. The debates which had taken place there had no "aim other than the discovery of the truth."

All the same, one ought never to forget that we are here dealing with the noble decline of a great state, not with its rise. The ideas of these "young" patricians did not lead to fruitful developments. If one thinks of their valiant fight, one is reminded of Lepanto, "of that all-devouring war against the Turks in 1570 and the following years." The war threw the republic into a "debt . . . which exceeded six million ducats," a debt which had been contracted at 14, 10, and 8 percent interest. Niccolò Contarini wrote in his *Historie Venetiane* that this had led to a situation which resembled a "desperate form of providence." Niccolò Contarini, the Doge who died of the plague on April 1, 1631, was a man of inflexible asceticism, rigid in his manners and in the defence of his political ideals. Although he never contemplated his age with optimism, he did not alter his plans and aspirations or those of his friends with the changing circumstances. He began the history of the city with the year 1597 and observed bitterly that "if there ever was an age in which truth was hated, considered dangerous and persecuted, it is the present age, in which not only rulers but also private people are so angry that they take up arms to make sure in every way that their defects are suppressed and the truth silenced." It was Contarini's intention to tell all "without passion and with an unmoved and truthful heart." There is no doubt that this cult of moral and religious values and the faith in the destiny of the republic and her ideals proves that men like Donà and Contarini were not victims of the decadence of which Croce spoke, that is of a decadence of moral enthusiasm. It is nevertheless clear that the drama of their lives bears witness to unfinished labours and to a battle lost.

We have spoken of Venice, the place where Galileo

spent happy years. Pisa and Padua, Tuscany and the Venetian lands—these are the geographical limits of his activities, with Rome and the post-Tridentine church in the background. Florence and Venice had been for several centuries the most brilliant centres of civilisation in Italy and Europe. For a long time they had been free republics, even though their regimes had differed. In both Venice and Florence people had borne witness ever since the fourteenth century to a civilisation renewed through the revival of antiquity. There had been a free circulation of ideas between these cities, and one ought not to forget that there had been a free exchange of teachers between the universities of Pisa and Padua and that such exchanges were still common at the time of Galileo. From Mercuriale to Liceti, from Libri to Berigardo, Pisa and Padua had had the same professors: they had gone from one place to the other in response to the highest stipends and the most favourable conditions offered.

Though centres of humanistic renewal, both Venice and Florence were replete with an intense religious spirit, in great need of a reform. Savonarola had come from Ferrara and made himself the prophet of an ecumenical mission in Florence. But he had always kept his eyes firmly fixed upon Venice, which he considered a model of civic government. He held it up as a symbol of neighbourliness in more senses than one. In tearful devotion to liberty, Florence had fought her last battle in the thirties. From then on all Florentine republicans had come to regard Venice as a last refuge and, like Donato Giannotti, had found there something like an image of civic rectitude and also something of that intense and austere religiosity of which Savonarola had dreamt. After the thirties, when Florentine republicanism was completely extinguished, the whole of life in Florence took on another form. Her cultural hegemony had come to an end some time ago. But now even civic life itself was grinding to a standstill. When Galileo told his friends that he was able to lead an authentic life only in the country he doubtless gave expression to a conventional attitude; but he also drew our attention to the crisis of city life which stemmed from both economics and politics. In Venice the people who had been "the first men of the sea" started to invest their money in land in the territories of Verona, Polesina, and lower Friuli. Through such ruralisation there came about something like a new feudal age. And this ruralisation was clearly due to the crisis in industry and commerce brought about by conservatism and by the inability to adapt old patterns of behaviour. The exaltation of rural life was a characteristic expression of this development. A contemporary biographer said of Galileo: "It seemed to him that in some way the city was the prison of the speculative mind and that the freedom of the countryside was the book of nature, always open to people who enjoyed reading and studying it with the eyes of the mind." These words complement the passage, so famous and so often quoted, from the *Dialoghi e dimostrazioni matematiche* about the Venetian arsenals. They too, at least in part, are the expression of a conventional feeling. But in the last analysis all these texts were an expression of the tensions caused by a decline which was not easily accepted, by the transformation of a whole form of life and the extinction of a vital spirit.[6] The physical circle within which Galileo spent

---

[6] V. Viviani, *Racconto istorico*, in Galileo, *Opere*, XIX, p. 626. On the Venetian arsenal, see *ibid.*, VIII, p. 49. A. Persiano, follower of Telesio and a member of the *Linceo*, who was acquainted with Galileo, began his *Trattato dell'ingegno dell'huomo*, Venice, 1576, with a description and praise of the Venetian mint, a marvel of technical organisation. Galileo's return to Florence and his decision to serve a re-

his life is something like a symbol of all this: it stretches from the years of freedom spent in Padua to the period spent in the voluntary service of the Grand Duke and leads to the sad imprisonment in Arcetri. His choice too was symbolic. He explained its motivation in a letter from Padua to Vincenzio Vespucci in 1609: "One does not get used to accepting stipends from a Republic, no matter how splendid and generous, without actually rendering a service to the public. For if one really wants to serve the public, one must really satisfy the public, not just one man. And as long as I am strong and capable of reading and working, no Republic in the world can free me from this duty, leaving me alone to enjoy the emoluments. All in all, this sort of thing I cannot accept from somebody other than an absolute prince." We are dealing here with a noble decline, especially in Venice. But no matter how noble, it was a decline, cultural as well as political and economic. It will be recalled that Galileo was born the year after the concluding session of the Council of Trent. In this respect it is worth while to follow minutely the functioning of censorship in Italy and the suppression of ideas through that instrument so admirably suited to the battle, the *Index*. It had been in operation for some time, not only to silence the voices of the dead but to extinguish at their very origin the voices of the living. The very first list of prohibited books, prepared by Paul IV in 1559, included all the works not only of Boccaccio, but also of Machiavelli, Erasmus, and even of the "sceptical mystifier Gelli." Preoccupied by their vision of the whole rather than with an analysis of actual events, historians have not thrown much light upon the rise of the *Index*. They

---

spected prince rather than a republic are too well known to deserve further discussion. They ought to be kept in mind, however, for an understanding of the mental climate of the age.

have not brought out the actual difference it made in each case in each place. They have thus failed to bring out the silent battles that were being fought behind the scenes about certain works, publishing houses, the sales and the circulation of books brought in from abroad. The barrier set up to the circulation of ideas was a hard one; and at times it was relentless. Everything vital and new that had been produced during a century and a half of cultural effort was now being mutilated and suppressed. Texts of such high artistic and historical value as Castiglione's *Courtier* and Guicciardini's *History* were quietly bowdlerised and transformed by the censors. All the sincerely open-minded thoughts on religion that had been produced by the age of humanism from Giannozzo Manetti, Aeneas Silvio Piccolomini, and Francesco Zabarella to Lorenzo Valla and Ludovico Vives were now crippled and prohibited. Platonism was stunted by the condemnation of Francesco Giorgio Veneto and Francesco Patrizi da Cherso. The study of ancient Jewish thought was crippled by the condemnation of the most adventurous of Renchlin's intellectual explorations. Given all this, the bare pages of the *Index* give only a pallid idea of the real battle with all its snares and miseries. As so often happens in periods of cultural suppression, personal enemies, dangerous rivals, and irritating colleagues were accused of a lack of religion. But above all such an accusation was likely to be raised against those who had new ideas which were bound to cause difficulties to men who were conservative simply because they were lazy.

The secret history of the great battle which was supposed to protect the Catholic world from the progress of European knowledge is still to be written. To a large extent this history is of particular interest to Italy. It is reflected in many textual problems of the great works of our literature. It is a history without which it is difficult to understand the atmosphere of suspicion, secretiveness, and suppression which dominated the world of culture in the age of Galileo. Everything became dangerous. The Commissioner of the Master of the Sacred Palace wrote from Rome that it had been discovered that even "ecclesiastical authors, even saints and doctors of the church whose works were printed in Bâle, Frankfurt, and other suspect places, had been infected by errors of the most important kind." Heresy was ferreted out from dictionaries and traced in the collections of apophthegms; it was believed to be hidden in the very names of the printers and had to be exterminated there. The censors scratched and cut the pages of the folio volumes printed in Bâle that were designed to announce to the world the conquests of the Italian Renaissance. There was never enough time, there were never enough men, to read, to purge, to destroy. There were never enough guardians. One of the many dispatches directed that "the greatest diligence is to be employed in watching . . . the approaches and gates of cities, with their couriers, carriers, and messengers" so that the vehicles of ideas, the books, may be stopped. The censors felt most uncomfortable and in order to gain a respite they demanded a long pause in printing. Manuscripts accumulated and in spite of great pressure from higher authorities, people had often to wait for a long time for a decision. The very flexibility and comprehensiveness of the criteria of censorship caused confusion; and it was always easier to ban than to expurgate. On July 26, 1614, Robert Bellarmine directed a very significant circular to the provincial inquisitors: "My father, the heretics and enemies do not tarry . . . to sow continuously their errors and heresies in the fields of Christendom. They write innumerable pernicious books and every day they send out new ones. It is vital for us not to sleep. We have to try to exterminate them at least in those places in which we can." This letter was written on December 13, 1613, a few months before the famous letter by Galileo to Benedetto Castelli, about the demarcation between the fields of scientific research and those of faith.

As if this were not enough the unrelenting repression often transformed itself into an instrument of private persecution, even in cases which had nothing much to do with the defence of religious values. An accusation of heresy was too convenient not to be used against a rival or a hated opponent propounding doctrines which in any way whatever might damage the sacred habits of men captive to their own laziness. Thus in spite of the sympathy of many ecclesiastical authorities, the death-knell tolled for the Platonism of Patrizi at the trial which began in 1592 and ended at the *Index* in 1596. And similarly, on Saturday, November 25, 1600, Cesare Cremonini, in the episcopal palace of Padua, in the office of the Holy Inquisition, signed the condemnation of Telesio's *De Rerum Natura Iuxta Propria Principia* because it contradicted the teachings of Aristotle's *Caesar Cremoninus, in Gymnasio philosophus ordinarius, manu propria*.[7] It is time we stopped thinking of Cremonini and his ilk as strong and liberal minds. They have acquired a reputation for liberalism because from time to time they allowed themselves to make fun of the friars who were actually much less prejudiced than they; for Bruno, Campanella, Paolo Sarpi, and Micanzio were, or had been, friars. The "heresy" of Cremonini was confined to Aristotelian rationalism. In the thir-

---

[7] On all this see Rotondò, *op. cit.*, and L. Firpo, "Filosofia italiana e Controriforma," *Rivista di filosofia*, 41, 1951, pp. 150–73 and 42, 1951, pp. 30–47. T. Gregory, "L'Apologia ad Censuram di Francesco Patrizi," *Rinascimento*, 4, 1953, pp. 89–104, and the same author's "L' 'Apologia' e le 'Declarationes' di F. Patrizi," in *Medioevo e Rinascimento*, Studies in honor of B. Nardi, Florence, 1955, pp. 387–424.

teenth century it may have been daring, but in the sixteenth century it was very much a commonplace. Historians who keep raving about the boldness of this Paduan Aristotelianism or Averroism would do well to reread Gualdo's often-quoted letters to Galileo about Cremonini. On May 6, 1611, Gualdo wrote from Padua: "I have talked at great length to Cremonini recently. He made fun of your observations and was greatly surprised that you took them to be true." And he went around laughing at what he called "the deception of the eye glasses." On July 20 Gualdo told the following story: "Recently, I saw the said Cremonini. I entered and discoursed of you and said to him, as a joke: 'Mr. Galilei is expecting with great trepidation the publication of your work.' He replied: 'He has no cause for trepidation, because I do not mention any of his observations.' I replied: 'It is enough if you hold in everything the opposite of him.' He rejoined: 'Of this you can be certain, because I do not wish to approve of things I have neither experienced nor seen.' I replied: 'This is precisely what displeases Mr. Galilei so much, that you have chosen not to see them.' He objected: 'I think there are other people who have not been able to see them either; and anyway to look through these glasses makes one's head spin.' I replied: 'You swear by the words of the master and you do well to follow hallowed antiquity.' Whereupon he burst out: 'O, how well would Mr. Galilei have done not to enter into such vagaries and not to leave the liberal atmosphere of the Paduan establishment.'" There was nothing personal in Cremonini's attack on Galileo. They had been colleagues and had remained friends, and had even helped each other with money. But Cremonini was argumentative, especially when challenged; and, above all, he did not want "flighty" speculations and did not want to make his head spin with new ideas which were far removed from Aristotle and his well-ordered little world in which everything was in its place or, if not, soon would be.[8] What he called the "liberal Paduan atmosphere" was a long way from the "free philosophising" for which Galileo, his friends and disciples (who included a great many friars who had learnt to deride Aristotelianism) were fighting. No matter how respectfully it treated the faith, it was no accident that the repression hit the new science—and all those honest researches which had caused a ferment and restlessness in the cloisters —much harder than it hit the erudite liberalism of the schools. That "liberalism" had been isolated and exorcised for centuries and had exhausted itself in those dialectical discussions *in utramque partem* of which Galileo spoke with lashing irony. It was no accident that the enemies of the new science obtained their ammunition from the dialectical arsenal of this so-called liberalism.[9]

If one peruses those first lists of prohibited books, one will notice immediately that together with the works of people who had rebelled against the church, a great many important products of the Renaissance were condemned. These works stood in opposition to the teachings of the universities which, all in all, had defended the ancient traditions. In their courses

---

[8] Gualdo's letter is in Galileo, *Opere*, XI, pp. 99-101 and 65-66. Cremonini's work, *Disputatio de Coelo*, Venice, 1612, was actually published in 1613. In November, 1612, Pignoria wrote to Galileo (*Opere*, XI, p. 436) that the book was printed but that it had been decided to enlarge the type because it was such a small booklet. On September 28, 1613, Sagredo finally sent it to Galileo. Cp. A. Favaro, "Cesare Cremonini e lo studio di Padova," *Archivio Veneto*, Series II, 5, pt. II, 1883, pp. 430-50.

[9] Cp. *Opere*, I, p. 412; IV, p. 248. For a critique of the debates *ad utramque partem* see Campanella, *Lettere*, p. 245. In his notes to the *Esercitazioni* by Rocco, Galileo, *Opere*, VII, p. 629, distinguished sharply between rhetorical, dialectical discourse and scientific discourse. He considered the distinction absolute.

on philosophy the universities had upheld if not the
whole of Aristotle, at least the use of this or that
Aristotelian text. And by philosophy was meant, of
course, physics, cosmology, and psychology.

In order to avoid an argument about the meaning
of words, it is well to remind ourselves that the
renewal of reading and of methods of study, the
whole reorientation of thought and the enlargement
of the intellectual horizon which we are wont to name
metaphorically "the Renaissance" or perhaps, more
equivocally, "humanism," had taken place outside the
universities. It had concerned, in the main, fields and
disciplines which were, at best, marginal to traditional
studies and had been considered of minor importance.
This point is too often overlooked. From the fourteenth to the sixteenth century the new culture had
neither taken its momentum from the universities nor
triumphed there. And when it did penetrate the universities, it did so only marginally. The centres of the
new knowledge were the cloisters and the chancell-
ies, princely courts and academies, that is, the free
assemblies of learned men. Fruitful restlessness was
introduced into the universities by the masters of
grammar and rhetoric, perhaps even by the masters
of logic and ethics or by the professors of Greek.
But neither Petrarch nor Cusanus, neither Ficino nor
Pico, neither Alberti nor Toscanelli had been university teachers. True, Poliziano was a university
teacher, but of rhetoric and logic, i.e. of one of the
minor disciplines. Plato and the more important commentaries on Aristotle had been introduced through
instruction in Greek. And such essential instruments
of the new science as Archimedes wormed their way
into the universities through the activities of Greek
scholars, through the initiative of a Maecenas or the
curiosity of an encyclopaedist like Valla. In fact
Valla owned that ancient codex of Archimedes from
which all the many copies and translations and edi-

tions of the sixteenth century were made.[10] As a
whole the universities opposed all new knowledge
even when it sailed under the colours of antiquity.
But gradually the echoes of the new departures in
knowledge could be heard indirectly even inside the
established schools. To teach meant to read and com-
mentate on ancient authors. And the time-honoured
author in logic, ethics, and natural philosophy was
Aristotle. In the teaching of the arts faculties in the

---

[10] It is strange that many scholars, when discussing Galileo's
knowledge of Archimedes, refer only to the translations and
editions of Archimedes in print and forget the many manuscripts in circulation in the fifteenth century. The ms. here
referred to is now lost. It was used by Valla in *De expetendis
et fugiendis rebus*, Venice, 1501. It was the great encyclopaedia, the scientific parts of which were of the greatest
importance even if not all historians seem to be aware of this.
But see G. McColley, "G. Valla: An un-noted advocate of the
Geo-Heliocentric Theory," *Isis*, XXXIII, 1941, pp. 312–14,
and the precious researches published between 1894 and 1898
by J. H. Heiberg. Valla's codex came into the hands of
Alberto Pio da Carpi. According to Heiberg and Heath it
was the source for the *Laurenziano* and the *Parigini*, which
were considered the most authoritative ones for the reconstitu-
tion of the text. It is interesting to note that the *Laurenziano*
was copied in 1491 by Lorenzo de' Medici at the suggestion of
Poliziano. Jacobus Cremonensis' version, promoted by Pope
Nicholas V, it seems, was made from Valla's codex. Bessarion
owned a Greek Archimedes, and an *exemplar vetus* of the
Greek text, according to Regiomontanus, was *apud magistrum
Paulum*, who according to Heiberg and Heath is to be
identified as the monk Paolo Albertini of Venice. According
to others, he was, more plausibly, Paolo Toscanelli with whom
Regiomontanus was acquainted and whom he considered one
of the greatest mathematicians of his time. This latter sup-
position is all the more plausible since the copy of Regiomontanus' Latin version was completed about 1461, i.e. at a time
when we have documentary evidence of his scientific relations
with Toscanelli, i.e. *magister Paulus*. On all this see now M.
Clagett, *Archimedes in the Middle Ages*, Vol. I, Madison,
Wisconsin, 1964.

fifteenth century there loomed, above all, the study of philosophy, which meant in Padua the commentary on several books of the *Physics*, of *De Generatione et Corruptione*, of *De Anima*, and of *De Coelo et Mundo*. For preparatory studies people used courses in logic; and this meant a commentary on the *Prior* and the *Posterior Analytics* and courses in ethics, which meant a commentary on the *Nicomachean Ethics*. When required there were minor courses such as courses on "sophistics," i.e. the commentaries on the *Elenchi Sofistici*. They attracted both attention and interest. The masters of Merton College for instance managed to spread the taste for logic from Oxford, and the same taste was stimulated by the *Calculationes*, which were destined to have a decisive influence on physics and finally even on metaphysics and theology. With all this, the humane disciplines were taken up again. And these disciplines, linked as they were to a new and more ample knowledge of ancient texts, especially of Greek texts (due to the expertise of grammarians, philologists, and rhetoricians), succeeded in affecting the balance inside the schools, even though they had their centre of gravity outside these schools. They made the new masters turn handsprings and gave prominence to subjects which until then had occupied a very secondary or purely preliminary position. It was natural that in a school whose curriculum was based upon commentaries on ancient texts, the Greek scholar who was able to translate the Greek philosophers and the Greek physicians and their hitherto mainly unknown works directly from the original Greek should begin to occupy a very prominent position. The grammarian who could read Euclid, Apollonius, Archimedes, Strabo, Ptolemy, and Galen ended up by giving lectures to physicians, logicians, and physicists. When Galileo studied medicine in Pisa the *Parva Naturali* were read in Niccolò Leonico Tomeo's translation and with his commentary. He was a man greatly

admired by Erasmus.[11] On the other hand, even a
student of philosophy who continued, as he ought to,
to confine himself to the old type commentary on
Aristotle, could not easily ignore the problems raised
by the circulation of new works, even when the
study of such works had been started by the grammarians. The instruction in the techniques of speech
and oratory were in general linked to the study of
morals and politics, and was carried out by those
men of letters who had initiated and been responsible
for the transformation of all the humane studies
(*studia humanitatis*). It therefore so happened that
in the chairs of natural philosophy or physics, cosmology and psychology the old tradition became petri-
fied, while the cultural reorientation was free to
crystallise around the disciplines of logic, morals,
politics, history, and literature. In these disciplines
people still spoke of Aristotle; but their commentaries
became rich in variations, now Platonic, now Epicurean. All these different theories began to be treated
historically. The result was that Aristotle lost his
monopoly. Plato and the Platonists, Socrates and the
Socratics, the ancients (that is the naturalists), the
atomists, if they were not actually used as text-books
in class, came in for discussion and comment. And
finally, in the second half of the sixteenth century,
we actually find readers of Plato, like Francesco
Patrizi da Cherso; or, in Pisa, Jacopo Mazzoni di
Cesena, the teacher and friend of Galileo. Officially

---

[11] The writer availed himself of, among other things, a
group of medical and physical texts in his possession. These
texts belonged to Ottavio Pellegrini, a physician in Volterra in
1594. The numerous and ample notes of Pellegrini reflect the
Pisan lectures. Among the books used there was, above all, the
Parva Naturalia, edited by Leonico Tomeo. The lack of
references to the conditions of university teaching is the cause
of many inaccuracies in Pio Paschini, *Vita e opere di Galileo
Galilei*, Città del Vaticano, 1964. (It appeared when the present
pages were already in print.)

the latter was Reader in philosophy, i.e. of Aristotle, but unofficially he was a Reader of Plato.

In the fifteenth century Plato, Plotinus, Proclus, and even Archimedes had been read outside the universities. They had been studied in academies, in such private institutions as the Ficinian Academy. These "Platonists" were by no means averse to Aristotelian morals and logic, for they thought them to be close to the morals and logic of Plato. But they also engaged in a spirited defence of the first naturalists, the Pythagoreans and Democritus (whom they admired and knew through Lucretius), against Aristotelian criticism. At times they assimilated Democritus to Pythagoras and even to Plato because they managed to equate atoms with numbers and elementary bodies. On this last point, we have not only Jacopo Mazzoni,[12] whose ideas had a direct bearing upon those of Galileo, but also the testimony of Niccolò Gherardini about Galileo. And Gherardini's testimony was amply confirmed by Galileo himself. "He praised several works by Aristotle and above all the writings on rhetoric and ethics and said that on those matters, he (Aristotle) had written admirably. He praised Plato sky-high for his golden eloquence and for his method of writing and composing dialogues. Above everybody else he praised Pythagoras for the way he had philosophised; but in sheer genius he held Archimedes to have surpassed everybody,

---

[12] J. Mazzoni, *In universam Platonis et Aristotelis philosophiam praeludia*, Venice, 1597, p. 189c. Mazzoni, quoting a passage by Proclus on *Timaios*, attributes to Plato not only the distinction between primary and secondary qualities but also a sort of corpuscular theory, placing Plato in line with the atomists. It is known that Galileo in a letter of May 30, 1597, to Mazzoni, not only declared himself in favour of Copernicus but also recalled the lively discussions he had had in Pisa with Mazzoni. He was glad that his friend and master had, at least in part, changed his mind.

and he called him his teacher."[13] One must emphasise Gherardini's statement. Galileo's preferences reflect the position assumed by a large body of the most open minded scholars of the sixteenth century—a position which had been the outcome of the most lively discussions of the preceding century. That is, they had all agreed to make use of Aristotle's morals and rhetoric and, in part, of his logic. They had added to this a liberal interpretation of Plato, the naturalists, and Archimedes—and they had adopted the habit of calling all this Platonism. The anti-Aristotelianism which was so rampant outside the established schools and universities amounted only to a denial of Peripatetic physics and especially of the inextricable connection between Peripatetic physics and metaphysics cultivated in the universities. It was this connection that was the butt of the violent attacks; and it was precisely this aspect of Aristotle, and this aspect alone, that the professors continued to defend from the chairs of philosophy.

For all this I do not mean to take sides in the debate on Galileo's Platonism and his opposition to Aristotle. These debates are very fashionable today, but never

---

[13] Niccolò Gherardini, *Vita di Galileo*, in: Galileo, *Opere*, XIX, p. 645. Viviani, XIX, p. 616, states that Galileo intended to imitate Plato in the form of the dialogue. It is not necessary to emphasise how important this testimony is in connection with *de interpretatione*. It is important to recall that the Venetian edition of 1540 of Ammonio's commentary was among Galileo's books (Cp. A. Favaro, "La libreria di G. G., descritta ed illustrata," *Bullettino di bibliografia e di storia delle scienze matematiche e fisiche*, Vol. XIX, 1886, pp. 219–93). Speaking of Galileo's books it is worth mentioning that he owned together with the works of Plato in Ficino's version, two copies of Lucretius, the minor works of Leonico Tomeo, Proclus' comment on Plato, Apollonius, and Archimedes. He also owned a copy of Sebastian Basson (1621), not to mention Borri, Alessandro Piccolomini, Della Porta, Cardano, Gassendi, and Fludd.

reach a high level. It is merely my intention to throw
some light on the situation which had developed
during the fifteenth and sixteenth centuries as a result
of the tension between the universities and the mental
climate outside them. The tension ended up by affecting the universities on the inside; and, no matter
how slowly, they experienced a crisis in the balance
of their courses. For the introduction of new texts
began eventually to shake the ancient authorities.
During the sixteenth century there spread both inside
and outside the universities a tendency towards com-
piling concordances. One of the centres of this activity had been Florence. The compilers used Plato's
metaphysics and Aristotle's physics. True, it had not
been easy to detach Peripatetic physics from its
presuppositions and separate it from its metaphysical
implications. There had, in fact, arisen something like
a doctrine of two truths. One and the same teacher
had come to profess Peripateticism from his chair
and Platonism among his cultivated friends. And all
this at a time—and this ought not to be forgotten—
at which Peripateticism represented tradition, and
Platonism reform and renewal. Platonism, as happened
in more than one case, could even become united to a
Lucretian vision of nature.[14]

---

[14] These points of view were often baffling and the classifications introduced by the manuals are of no real help. Hence
it is expedient to insert subdivisions into the great currents
though they are only partially valid. Thus there is something
to be said for the distinction introduced by A. Koyré between
Platonism as mathematicism and Platonism as mysticism. It
has met with a fair response. Koyré grasped very well the
significance and the polemical intent of mathematical Platonism
as opposed to Aristotelian empiricism (*Études galiléenes*, III,
Paris, 1939, p. 269: "The use of mathematics in physics *is*
Platonic—even if it is unknown"). But he did somewhat obscure
the manner in which the two types of Platonism were mixed up
with one another, even in Galileo. On the other hand one
ought to pay attention to Marcello Palingenio Stellato of whom

In this respect the situation of the universities in Pisa and Padua at the time of Galileo is very instructive. When Galileo was a student of medicine at Pisa, Cesalpino was teaching medicine there. The chairs of philosophy were occupied by Borri, an Aristotelian physicist, and by Verino, who had strong ethical and aesthetic interests and whose efforts to reconcile different doctrines were governed by Platonic tendencies. Then there was Libri, the logician. He was a Peripatetic of the strictest observance and was to become a fervent enemy of Galileo in Padua. In 1589 Galileo became Reader in mathematics with a stipend of sixty florins. At that time there were several professors of philosophy. There was first Mazzoni, a man keen on concordances. Officially he was a Peripatetic; unofficially he was a Platonist. His

---

Koyré speaks with much eloquence in *From the Closed World to the Infinite Universe*, New York, 1958, pp. 24–27. With him the tangle became very complicated because of the intrusion of Lucretian and Epicurean elements, as had happened also in Ficino.

One should not forget the spirited sixteenth-century discussions between mathematicians and logicians about the reducibility of mathematical procedures to Aristotelian terms. To remain in a Galilean circle, we have here P. Catena, who was professor in Padua from 1547 to 1577; F. Barozzi, probably a colleague of Catena and translator of Proclus' comment on Euclid and author of *quaestio de certitudine mathematicarum* (1560); Alessandro Piccolomini, who was attacked by Barozzi and who defended the superiority of logic. Clavio, in his *Euclide*, in the commentary on the first problem, declared that the attempts to reduce mathematical formulations to the syllogism were useless. There is a reference to this in N. W. Gilbert, *Renaissance Concepts of Methods*, New York, 1960, pp. 90–91. But one will never understand the problem of Galileo's "method" correctly if one does not first examine the discussions on Galileo, in which (and this was no accident) the teachers of mathematics (and astronomy) were engaged. As a contemporary observed, at the bottom of the problem was the question whether mathematics is a science.

stipend amounted to five hundred florins. (Cesalpino, the physician, received four hundred florins.) Then there were Buonamici, Verino, and Libri.[15] In Padua

---

[15] Giulio Libri, born in Florence about 1550, was professor in Pisa. At first a professor "extraordinary," he later became a rival of Buonamici. After many bitter fights he went to Padua in 1595. He remained there until 1600, when he returned to Pisa to die there in December 1610. On December 17 Galileo wrote to Gualdo, not without cruel irony: "There died in Pisa the Philosopher Libri, a bitter opponent of my many vagaries. Since he never wanted to see their truth on earth, he might now see their truth as he is passing into heaven." Sassetti's letter of November 22, 1570, to Lorenzo Giacomini, is proof of the reputation Libri enjoyed: "That Mr. Giulio de' Libri used everything he knew in order to prove to people that he knew nothing" (F. Sassetti, *Lettere edite ed inedite*, Florence, 1855, p. 8; for a comment by Libri on a sonnet by I. Martelli see ms. Magliab., IX, 139, and for two lectures on philosophy, Ambrose, Q. 122 sup.). As to the other professors mentioned above there was, apart from Mazzoni, the well-known Francesco de' Vieri (Verino the Second), author of numerous works, including works on the philosophy of nature, on Christian Platonism, on aesthetic and moral matters, and on Platonic topics. All too well known, there was Cesalpino; but in speaking of Galileo one ought to pay closer attention to him than one is wont to. In a letter written to Galileo sometime in 1615 or 1616, perhaps by Paolo Antonio Foscarini (*Opere*, XII, p. 216), we read that the Copernican theory, or better, the theory of the motion of the earth, could be supported by the "consensus of many ancient and modern philosophers, among whom there ought to be included Peripatetics like Cusanus, an excellent mathematician, Celio Calcagnino, a man versed in everything, and Andrea Cesalpino, a modern philosopher." Galileo himself, writing in 1632 to Cesare Marsili on the *Discourses* of Roffeni, distinguished between his theory of the earth's motion as the cause of the tides, and that of Cesalpino.

Girolamo Borri from Arezzo was born in 1515. Philosopher and physician, he taught in Rome, Paris, Siena, Pisa, and Perugia. He was several times in Pisa and always involved in violent quarrels. His licence was from Pisa, but he died in Perugia, August 26, 1592. Galileo knew and discussed both his

in 1592 the philosophers were Cremonini, a convinced and strict Peripatetic, and Francesco Piccolomini from Siena, a secret Platonist who compiled, under a variety of names, Platonic treatises for young Venetian patricians of progressive ideas. Logic was taught by Petrella, an Aristotelian, a very modest man of Tuscan origin.[16] One can easily see how careful

---

De motu gravium et levium, Florence, 1575, and his Dialogo del flusso e reflusso del mare, edited and corrected several times between 1561 and 1577.

Buonamici will be discussed below. It is to be remembered that he gave courses on elementary logic to jurists at Pisa. See ms. Magliab., VIII, 49, which contains a treatise on syllogisms.

[16] There is no need to dwell on Cremonini. The case of Francesco Piccolomini is, however, significant. He was born in Siena in 1522. He was professor in Macerata and in Perugia and from 1560 onwards he held a chair in Padua (until he was almost eighty). Then he retired to Siena where he died in 1604. He was an opponent of Zabarella and the author of noteworthy writings on natural philosophy and on morals. Already his contemporaries attributed to him the ten books of Academicae contemplationes, published first in Venice in 1576 and then in Bâle in 1590 as the alleged work of the patrician Stefano Tiepolo. They also attributed to him the seven books of Peripateticae de anima disputationes, which were published in Venice in 1575 under the name Pietro di Francesco Duodo. Connected with Contarini, he was acquainted with Galileo, whose departure from Padua he, as Riformatore dello Studio, was to have cause to regret. As far as Piccolomini was concerned, it is interesting that he was a Platonist in private and that he had connections with the young Venetian patricians and their cultural education. It is no less interesting that the same Piccolomini reported in his Libri ad scientiam de natura attinentes (1596) the criticism levelled by "several mathematicians" against the motion of heavy bodies. By "several mathematicians" he seems to have meant Bradwardine and the calculatores, but also Galileo who as a mathematician had been his colleague for several years

one has to be not to contrast the university of Padua with that of Pisa, and how one must refrain from making too rigid a distinction between Platonic and Aristotelian professors. Galileo's career was a marginal case, for he taught mathematics, i.e. he commented on Euclid, the mechanics of Aristotle, on the *Sfera* and the *Theoria Planetarum.* The latter became more and more fundamental until in the end they took the place of philosophy. The sixty florins of 1589, the hundred and eighty florins of 1592, were quite a fat salary for a mere mathematician. And in 1609 Galileo's salary rose to one thousand florins. In 1610, in a letter to Belisario Vinta, Galileo made it a condition of his return to Tuscany that he should be known not only by his official title of mathematician but also by that of philosopher. One might think that the problem of the official designation was a matter of secondary importance. But in reality it was a question of principle and, perhaps, the birth of a new philosophy. Two centuries earlier, a whole new culture and a new conception of the world had turned upon the meaning of the expression *Studia Humanitatis;* now it was concentrated on the notion of what constituted a mathematician. Each in its own way, the study of man and the sciences of nature, destroyed the

---

and who had been engaged for some time in attacks on Aristotelianism.

It is worth mentioning that Piccolomini's chair was offered to Buonamici. Buonamici wanted to know from Galileo something more precise about Padua, and whether the transfer might be agreeable. (Cp. *Opere*, X, p. 251; the year 1609 is erroneously given as the date of the letter. By that time Buonamici was dead and the succession to the chair of Piccolomini, who had died soon after Buonamici, was no longer in question.)

Then there was Bernardino Petrella da Borgo San Sepolcro. His works on logic are remembered only because he fought with Zabarella. But among his contemporaries he had the reputation of a great logician. Cp. Monsignor Girolamo De Sommaia, *Schede scelte*, ms. Magliab., VIII, 75, c. 39r.

hegemony of the metaphysical and theological teachings of the scholastic tradition.

If it is necessary for an understanding of Galileo to
keep in mind the general academic situation of his
age, it would be a great mistake to attempt to trace
the components of his own education back to this
situation. The universities, especially the schools of
philosophy, propagated nothing but an utterly exhausted tradition. The last great occasion for the
Italian schools had been the great debate raised by
Pomponazzi about the soul. But it had ended in
nothing but Byzantine subtleties, devoid of any bite.
Telesio's philosophy of nature had failed to conquer
the schools and, for that matter, not one of the truly
dynamic ideas of the fourteenth century had made
any impression on them. The situation in Padua, in
spite of what some historians claim, was not essentially
different from that of Pisa.

As far as Pisa is concerned, it is enough to read
Filippo Sassetti's letters to Lorenzo Giacomini. Sassetti was the biographer of Ferrucci, the great naviga-
tor and explorer of the eastern oceans who had been
a student in Pisa from 1570 onwards. He had the
same professors as Galileo and the same circle of
friends. Sassetti was a brilliant writer. He lived in
the house of Buonamici and gave us a desolate picture
of the men with whom Galileo came into contact.
Of Messer Guido de' Libri, Sassetti tells us somewhat
irreverently that in his lectures and seminars he had
done his best to prove that he knew nothing. The
reputation of the famous Ludovico Boccadiferro was
no better. Caponsacchi, a so-called follower of Ficino
was derided by the students. They called him Head-
in-the-sack (*Capo in sacco*) or Sack-on-the-head
(*sacco in capo*). And since the professors were devoid
of imagination, the lecture halls were devoid of students. At the end of November 1570, "Vesorino (the
Platonist) had no students; Buonamico, 12; Caponsacchi, 3 . . ." Much the same picture emerges from

the note-books of Girolamo da Sommaia. Girolamo da Sommaia was an old pupil of Salamanca but had taken his degree at Pisa. In 1614 he was to become Director of Studies. He often used expressions like the "doctorlets" of Pisa and expressed the view that university teaching was a profession which made people die early and in poverty. And frequently he referred to the teachers in a tone halfway between irony and depression. The title "Borro's dark track" sums up facetiously the weakness of Girolamo Borri's lectures on physics. Of Buonamici one remembered especially his attacks on the friars, including those on the memory of the great St. Thomas himself. Mazzoni had a tremendous reputation, and it was said that although "he was a man who had a very good memory and made a great splash when speaking . . . he was not as well grounded in philosophy as many people thought." These note-books are full of petty and bizarre squabbles; and there is a great deal of spite. But the over-all impression one gains from them is that the knowledge taught was a tired, used-up knowledge which found no echo anywhere.[17]

At that time even an educated man like Ciriaco Strozzi refused to receive Telesio in Florence. Strozzi maintained that Telesio was not yet in his sixties and was therefore too young for philosophy. In the last analysis the stage was dominated by the worn-out attempts at concordances between Aristotle and Plato. Said Strozzi by way of synthesis: Plato equals a disorderly Aristotle; and Aristotle, a Plato put in order.

In Padua, since the people concerned were in many cases the same, the atmosphere was in no way different. There were the same persons, the same words,

---

[17] Filippo Sassetti, *Lettere edite ed inedite*, pp. 5ff. Da Sommaia, *Schede*, c. 38 vff., is not much kinder; if he does not spare Mazzoni, he is downright rude about Borri, c. 74r. As far as Buonamici was concerned, Sassetti stressed that he was prejudiced.

the same attitudes. Pisa and Padua were remarkably similar. In Padua, the bitter irony of Sassetti was matched by the solemn dignity of Gianfrancesco Sagredo. In a letter of April 4, 1614, to Marco Welser, he drew, with unusually vigorous lines, a picture of the contrast between the Renaissance ideal of an educated man and a contemporary professor. The letter was occasioned by a debate with Schneider: "I wrote very modestly about his equations and I wrote the truth. He replied to my opinion with great heat and jumped to the wrong conclusion . . . I am a Venetian gentleman and have never ceased being a man of letters . . . I have no intention of advancing my fortunes and acquiring fame and renown through the understanding of philosophy and mathematics. I prefer to be renowned because of the integrity and good administration of the magistrates and the government of the Republic . . . My studies are concerned with those things which as a Christian I owe to God; and as a citizen to my country, as a nobleman to my house, as a friend to my friends, and as a gentleman and true philosopher to myself . . . And even if from time to time I indulge in scientific speculations, you must not believe that I ever presume to compete with the professors of science; and even less do I want to quarrel with them. I only do so in order to find some recreation for my soul, inquiring freely, absolved from any obligation and without ulterior wishes, into the truth of any proposition to which I have taken a fancy."[18]

The world of Sagredo was also the world of Galileo. Like Sagredo, Galileo was wont to philosophise in this free spirit. Philosophy, which in the fifteenth century had taken refuge among politicians and moralists, now sought asylum among physicists and mathematicians, or, more precisely, among those "heretics" who had been chased from all the schools.

---

[18] Galileo, *Opere*, XII, pp. 45–46.

With great insight Kepler, in his famous *Sidereus Nuncius,* compared Galileo not to contemporary university professors, but to Cusanus, Copernicus, and Bruno as well as to the ancient Greeks.[19] If one has to establish connections, they have to be sought in the direction of extra-scholastic philosophy, i.e. in the philosophy of nature of Telesio and Campanella and the indefatigable curiosity of Cardano and Della Porta.[20] Actually there are not many names to be linked with that of Galileo, and the few which can be linked with his have all been clearly indicated by him. Among the ancients, his true teacher was Archimedes. Among the moderns "our common teacher" was Copernicus. In his great dialogue, the participants were Kepler and Mersenne and, in the background, Gilbert and Gassendi, Descartes and Hobbes. The adversary was not Ptolemy, but Peripateticism seen as a mixture of physics and theology as woven by tradition into Christian doctrine.[21]

---

[19] For Kepler's text see Galileo, *Opere,* (esp. III, pp. 97–126; X, pp. 319–40) and J. Kepler, *Gesammelte Werke,* IV, Munich, 1941, and XVI, Munich, 1954, pp. 142, 166, for the famous opinions on Bruno.

[20] For a slightly superficial review of Galileo's connections with Bruno, Stigliola, Della Porta, and Campanella, see V. Spampanato, *Quattro filosofi napoletani nel carteggio di Galileo,* Portici, 1907. As to Telesio, he is mentioned by Galileo in *De Motu, Opere,* I, p. 414. In another place, during the debate with Grassi, he states that he had not read Telesio; but adds that those who oppose him, do not know him (VI, pp. 118, 236, 397–98). One must not forget Galileo's connections with Persio, a great follower of Telesio. The name of Del Cardano comes up in the debate with Grassi (VI, pp. 118–19, 236, 397–98).

[21] In 1633, on December 1, Paganino Gaudenzio, master of theology in the university of Pisa, in his address *De barbarie repellenda,* Pisa, 1634, stated on p. 7 that Aristotle was the harbinger of every truth. That fine theologian was prepared to accept Buonamici's judgments on the friars and the moder-

Here we have to face the question of the Galilean revolution and what, precisely, it amounted to in the history of thought. And it is here that we have to trace the paths by which it was accomplished. The notes he took as a young man show very clearly that Galileo was well acquainted with medieval Peripateticism. These notes have come down to us in his own hand. They have been edited, in part, by Favaro and have been assigned by him, with good reason, to the year 1584.[22] But the view that these notes refer solely to the lectures of Buonamici is not so convincing. Why should they not also refer to the lectures of Borri and Verino? The reasons culled from a comparison with *De Motu* are not compelling. Neither Favaro nor, more recently, Giacomelli, seems to have examined the matter with sufficient care. Published in 1591, the fat folio volume of the Pisan teacher carries a very precise testimony: the work was born, he declares, immediately after the heated discussions on

---

ate errors of Cremonini in order to overcome the crisis in Aristotelianism. His *De dogmatum Origenis cum Philosophia Platonis comparatione*, Florence, 1639, is very revealing in this respect.

[22] There exists no careful study of the notes of his youth, nor any analysis of the authors and texts quoted in them. Yet the matter is not without interest. There are the references to Flaminio Nobili, which define with some precision a cultural climate, not to mention a quotation from Crinito's *De honesta disciplina*, which one would hardly expect in a work on physics. But it proves that Galileo's library contained a copy of Crinito's book. What seems even more strange is Favaro's omission of the notes on logic, which are capable of affording us a rare insight. I plan to publish these notes from ms. *Gal.* 27, which appeared in the original, published by Favaro together with the notes. But how can one disregard the fact that the codex contains the treatise *de praecognitionibus* as well as discussions on mathematical demonstrations and physics? And how can one ignore the connections with similar sections in the writings on logic by Zabarella and Petrella?

motion which had taken place *the other day* in the university between students and teachers of various courses.[23] This indication bears out Galileo's own memory, recorded in the letter to Mazzoni in 1597. In this letter Galileo refers to the quiet but lively con-

---

[23] Koyré, *Études Galiléenes*, I, p. 11, n. 2, suggests that neither Favaro nor Wohlwill ever had the "courage to open the enormous volume (1011 pages in folio)." It is true that Koyré was the first to provide a sufficiently thorough analysis of the work, with long extracts (*loc. cit.*, pp. 11–41). All the same, a new reading might be fruitful, especially when linked with other writings of Galileo in Pisa, e.g. such as the work on meteors in ms. Magliab., XII, 29. *De Motu* is something like a *summa* of the teaching of Buonamici as expressed in *Francisci Buonamici Florentini e primo loco philosophiam ordinariam in Almo Gymnasio Pisano profitentis, de motu libri X*, Florence, 1591. The occasion for this publication was the Pisan controversy, as was clearly set out by Buonamici on Fol. 3. We have proof of Galileo's conversations with Mazzoni from 1590 as well as the famous letter from 1597. Galileo wrote about them to his father on November 15, and Guidobaldo del Monte wrote of them to Galileo on December 8, *Opere*, X, pp. 44–46. It is strange that Giacomelli, *Galileo Galilei giovane e il suo "de motu,"* Pisa, 1949, p. 21, maintains that "there . . . is no evidence at all of disputes and controversies between Galileo and his Pisan colleagues, except in the account of Viviani who, as usual, makes a travesty of the facts." Giacomelli was able to rely on the authority of Wohlwill, *Galilei und sein Kampf für copernicanische Lehre*, Vol. I, Hamburg and Leipzig, 1909, p. 114, who observed that if there had been any discussions between the young mathematician and his venerable philosophical colleagues, they would have left a trace. But the truth is that there are traces: there is the evidence from the friendly, but lively conversations with Mazzoni and in those parts of his work of 1597 in which Galileo reviewed the response evoked by these debates. There is also the evidence from Buonamici, who decided in 1591 to publish his work in response, as it were, to the difficulties experienced by the young people who attended his classes and those of his colleagues.

versations with the master from Cesena. A very conspicuous part of Mazzoni's major work is a very faithful, but unfortunately constantly ignored, record of these conversations.[24] On the other side, only certain passages of the *Iuvenilia* can be compared with the book by Buonamici, and even then there are hardly any precise similarities.[25] Even if we allow

---

[24] There is a whole group of writings by Mazzoni which ought to be examined in order to find out what response was aroused by his conversations with Galileo. They ought to be compared with the relevant passages in Buonamici's *De Motu*.

[25] The truth of the matter is that if Galileo's notes had been compared more carefully with Buonamici's texts and if other similar texts had also been examined, the dependence alleged by Favaro (and alleged ever since by many people who have simply repeated Favaro's thesis) would have revealed itself as being of a very general nature. This does not necessarily negate the possibility that we really are dealing here with courses given by Buonamici. One ought to recall that the *De Motu* by the Pisan teacher was written a few years after these courses were held and that it was probably the result of the stimulus received from the debates launched by the "mathematicians." It indicates the polemical nature of the times, and the battles fought against a more militant Aristotelianism. Perhaps it is useful to refer to the *Discorso intorno alle cose che stanno in su l'acqua*, the work of a more mature Galileo. It brings out, through the refutation of Buonamici's *De Motu*, the motives which had inspired Buonamici as well as Galileo's own attitude: "It is not because of a mere caprice or because I have not read or understood Aristotle that I differ, at times, from him. Rather, it is because reason persuades me; and the same Aristotle has taught me that the intellect ought to settle for that which reason teaches . . . and Alcinous' opinion that philosophy ought to be free, is most true." By contrast there was the kind of research dominated by preconceived ideas, a research which followed the example of the same Aristotle, who often enough reveals "the will to overthrow Democritus [or others] . . ." Thus Buonamici in *De Motu* is too concerned with the refutation of the ancients, be it Plato or Archimedes. Galileo's text of

this question to be undecided, there can be no doubt that Galileo was well acquainted with all the Peripatetics' discussions about natural and violent motion and the motion of the heavens. It is clear that these discussions were his point of departure. The majority of the historians of modern science, Frenchmen, Germans, Englishmen, and Americans and unfortunately also, Italians, have persuaded themselves that almost all the initial ideas of Galileo or, at least, the critical arguments used by him, were due either to the physicists of Paris, to Albert of Saxony and the discussions influenced by him, or to the English *calculatores* or theoreticians of *de proportionibus velocitatum in motibus*. Each historian's preference seems to have been dictated by his own nationality. In this connection one ought to remember an old saying of Comte, emphasised by Vailati, that there is no point in a criticism unless the criticised hypothesis is replaced by another. Now it is undeniable that the physicists of the late middle ages, when they took up arguments used by ancient commentators, brought about a crisis in several of Aristotle's teachings. It may well be true that the theories about impetus, taking their cue from Filopono, demolished the theory that the means are the cause of motion. In spite of this there is no denying that all the many views capable of being considered as precursors of the views of Galileo appear as such only when torn from their contexts. While they are evidence that a certain amount of erosion of some Aristotelian views had taken place, none of them can be looked upon as capable of renewing the method of research, of destroying the ancient assumptions, or of rising above the ancient assumptions by giving birth to an entirely

---

1612 refers us to *La bilancetta* and again invites us to re-examine with a mind to more exact historical placement the conversation between Galileo and the Pisan philosophers, which had begun at least as early as 1590.

ew theory. All we have before Galileo are single "pieces" of criticism. They were destined to remain terile because they did not cause the abandonment either of the general assumptions or of the methods of nquiry. It is important to emphasise that even the most marvellous efforts of late medieval physicists emained imprisoned in the Aristotelian framework nd in its equivocations.[26] Even the researches of Benedetti, a pupil of Tartaglia, published in Turin n 1585, did not go further than the demolition of solated Aristotelian doctrines. This much was well rought out by Vailati. The one remarkable fact is hat a pupil of Tartaglia should have used Archimedes. Benedetti's writings were never referred to by Galileo, but it is certain that they were known to him.[27]

If Galileo was able by this road to arrive at his first bservations about the way in which bodies fall and t his refutation of the Aristotelian theory about otion in a vacuum, the decisive revolution took lace only when the whole established cosmology was urned upside down through his acceptance of a new heory of the universe. The transformation of his

---

[26] It is the great merit of Koyré (cp., however, M. Boas, *The Scientific Renaissance, 1450–1630*, London, 1962) to have ressed the change of perspective and mental climate in alileo. On the other hand a perusal of such worthy works s Curtis Wilson, *William Heytesbury. Medieval Logic and the ise of Mathematical Physics*, Madison, 1960, and H. Lamar rosby, *Thomas Bradwardine. His "Tractatus de proportioni- us." Its Significance for the Development of Mathematical hysics*, Madison, 1955, shows how little was contributed by ertain medieval disputes to the work of Galileo. One ought pay close attention to the note on the "precursors" by A. oyré, *La révolution astronomique*, Paris, 1961, p. 79.

[27] On Benedetti the pages by Vailati, "Le speculazioni di iovanni Benedetti sul moto dei gravi," *Atti dell'Accademia elle scienze di Torino*, 33, 1897–98, are very important. As ated, Galileo does not appear to have mentioned Benedetti. ut he was discussed several times by Mazzoni.

thought was not caused by a number of separate reasons and experiments (many of which may not even have been carried out by him) but by a general and completely novel hypothesis about the cosmic system. It happened when the Copernican theory was joined, in Galileo's mind, to the Archimedean method. This revolution enabled him to face the problems of physics without the trammels of Peripateticism. Galileo's letters to Mazzoni of May 30, 1597, and to Kepler of August 4 of the same year are the telling documentation of this "mental revolution." In these letters he not only defends Copernicus, but he also says that it was precisely Copernicus' view, accepted for many years (*multis abhinc annis*), that had made it possible for him to discover the causes of natural phenomena otherwise inexplicable. There is some doubt as to how Galileo managed to convince himself that he had demonstrated the Copernican theories. What matters, however, is that it was not a question of his acceptance of an astronomical hypothesis but that of his acceptance of a new way of seeing the world. This new way stood at the end of a long line of theories which, though formulated outside the field of science, had nevertheless been determined by the progress of science. If one reads Copernicus' *De Revolutionibus Caelestibus* in its original autograph version, even complete with those parts that were later deleted by the author himself, one cannot fail to see that it is but the last in a long line of writings about the sun composed during the fifteenth century.[28] Underlying these observation

---

[28] Nikolaus Kipernikus, *Gesamtauagabe*, Vols. I–II, Munich 1944–49 (the first volume contains a reproduction of the autograph). Cp. Vol. II, pp. 30–31. See also the pregnant observations by Koyré, *op. cit.*, p. 15. Perhaps one ought also to note the attack on Copernicus by the theoreticians of the "precursors." Interesting points are to be found in N. R. Hanson, "The Copernican Disturbance and the Keplerian Revolu-

and arguments, and in some cases prior to them, was a unified vision of the world, shaped by the confluence of many philosophical intuitions by no means free from mystico-religious ideas. This was an instance of a radical "subversion" of the vision of the cosmic order similar to the one which was to arouse the enthusiasm of Bruno.

It was indeed an entirely new way of looking at the relationship between the heavens and the earth, between man and matter. It was so revolutionary a vision, and its consequences so far-reaching, that even today it is difficult to fathom. As a result of it, precisely at the moment that man had seemed to understand himself in all his actual power, anthropocentrism was destroyed. Perhaps it is better to say that at the very moment at which the anthropocentric myth fell there asserted itself, with a liberating impulse, the recognition of the value of human work as something which was not yet, but could one day become, the effective source of new speculations and constructions.[29]

In 1597 Galileo was in fact in a position similar to that of Bruno. Bruno considered Copernicus' theory to be not a mathematical hypothesis capable of "saving" the appearances of phenomena but a vision of reality altogether free from Aristotelian presuppositions. At bottom all his criticism was and remained a criticism of Peripateticism—not of Ptolemy. He criticised a certain conception of reality: not an astronomi-

---

ion," *Journal of the History of Ideas*, XXII, 1961, pp. 169–84. Hanson distinguishes between philosophical cosmology and technical astronomy and observes that *qua* technical astronomy the work of Copernicus could conceivably have been written immediately after Ptolemy's mathematical syntax. He adds that there never was a Ptolemaic *system* of astronomy and that it was Copernicus who *invented* a systematic astronomy.

[29] Koyré, *op. cit.*, p. 75, observes correctly that "geocentrism does not imply an anthropocentric conception of the world."

cal hypothesis. And it was this new conception which provided the intellectual framework which eventually made it possible to abandon the whole circle of Aristotelian views on motion, space, gravity, quality, and matter. It is no accident that Mazzoni's work of 1597 contains in the parts connected with the discussion on Galileo, a theory of corpuscles arrived at by a strange combination of Democritus and Plato. It also contains an assertion which followed from it and which was to be given greater precision by Galileo, the assertion that all secondary qualities are subjective in contrast to the geometrical nature of primary qualities.

At the same time, Galileo went beyond Aristotelianism and set out his Archimedean method. It was founded on an elaboration of the concepts of space and motion and on the assumption that mathematical language was functional and an adequate instrument for the exploration of the reality of nature. This does not mean that he held that one could construct *a priori* the whole web of the universe—this, he thought, was something for God and not man. It meant that in the physical field mathematics was to be accepted as a valid language, objectively linked to the structure of things. Unfortunately here too, as with the "system" of the world, historians, and especially those historians of science who are intent upon defending "continuity," account for everything that was revolutionary in Galileo's thought by confining it to a few dents he managed to make in the commonplaces of the teaching of the schools. They stress that he did uphold the value of Aristotelian logic both in the sphere of rhetoric and that of the moral sciences. But the truth is that Galileo believed that the instrument with which one can understand nature, the logic of the sciences, is mathematics and mathematics alone. Hence his double judgment on Aristotle: harshly negative in regard to physics because of his ignorance of mathematics; strongly positive in morals and in everything that belongs to the analysis of discourse between human beings.

Given this picture, the acceptance of the Copernican conception of the world represents without doubt Galileo's connection with the philosophies of the sixteenth century, Bruno included. Hence also Galileo's preoccupation with ideas of a strictly Platonic character. This preoccupation was to last down to 1638, the year of the *Dialoghi*. It cannot be separated from the main body of his doctrines, and it accounts for the long disquisitions on the soul as the divine seat of light and on the manner in which the solar system is constituted in regard to the concentration and expansion of primeval light. It also accounts for his theory of *spiritus*, the soul of the world, of the nourishment of the sun and of universal life. Disquisitions of this kind are to be found throughout Galileo's works. They serve a double purpose: first of all, they show how he himself understood Copernicus and what Copernicus meant to him. Secondly, they show that Galileo, threatened by his Peripatetic opponents, in order to defend himself against their metaphysics, had recourse to a metaphysics of his own. This metaphysics was the one that had sustained the *De Revolutionibus*—one that was by no means out of favour in certain religious circles. There is, for instance, a letter to Pietro Dini, written on March 26, 1615. To a large extent it could have been written by any follower of Ficino, for it contains long quotations from the Pseudo-Dionysius, not one of the authors most frequently used by Galileo. It gives the impression that he sought metaphysical help at any price in a doctrine which was not even organically linked to his own work. For we must never forget that by that time he had openly accepted Gassendi's refutation of Fludd's doctrines.

Between 1609 and 1610 Galileo went through a new development. Until that time he had been predominantly preoccupied with the problems of motion and with a general theory of reality as matter, of nature incapable of deceiving or of being deceived by machines because it obeys laws which are both rigorous and ascertainable. Copernican theory had been his horizon, and his mind had worked within the frame set by that theory. It had brought about that "revolution" in theory without which neither techniques nor instruments nor experimental data are of any use. But the construction of the telescope and, in January 1610, the discovery of the satellites of Jupiter followed step by step by the observation of the three bodies of Saturn, of the solar spots and the phases of Venus, directed his mind towards a cosmology. It was then that he transformed the Copernican vision from a general concept into a rigorous system in which sensuous experiences were integrated with the help of mathematical demonstration. And it was then that Copernican theory ceased to be a general philosophy of the type taught by Bruno and a mere presupposition of experience. It became a verified theory capable of further verification, and at that moment Galileo felt himself to be a philosopher in an entirely new sense. He was now a philosopher who had actually *seen* that the world was not the world of Aristotle, who had seen *new* heavens. As a student of motion he had been destined by God, as Paolo Sarpi put it, to define the universal laws of motion and to reduce the whole world of life, and even psychic phenomena as well, as acts of the will to them. But now his grasp of the reciprocal relationship between sensuous experiences and exact demonstration made him more aware of reality and its many appearances. He now saw the structure of reality and the foundations of objectively valid mathematics, the limits as well as the value of human knowledge, clearly revealed. As a result he disentangled the misunderstandings which the Peripatetic confusion between physics and theology had introduced into the field of religion. He saw that human knowledge is valid in proportion to the extent to which it takes into account its own limitations—that is, the limits of its verifiability. It is real knowledge when it is knowledge of real things, and then it is not merely a mathematical hypothesis designed to make appearances look real.

With these insights, the Copernican vision divested itself of its metaphysical and mythical implications. In writing to Cesi, Galileo wrongly defended its errors; but he did so in the name of the obedience that philosophy owes to reality, in the name of a philosophy that is sensitive to the nature of things.

As knowledge of the finite based on mathematics and experience, philosophy was thus detached from faith. There were two books, two languages, two ways of reading them. Faith was based upon other exigencies and existed on a different plane—it could not be touched by science. Science neither supports nor denies it; it is not a substitute, neither is it a confirmation nor a falsification. Philosophy is of the earth; it is limited but in constant progress; and, above all, it is human. It is a worldly knowledge of worldly things, capable of verification, but also fallible and capable of progress. On the physical horizon there appear no incorruptible heavens and none of the eternal motions of the stars of which Aristotelian theology was so fond. The whole sphere of human knowledge is earthly and subject to change. It is both limited and conscious of its limitation. Deprived of transcendental presences, mundane science recognises the existence of another kind of experience: faith. There can be no conflict between the two once the Aristotelian confusion between physics and theology is eliminated. It is precisely here that Galileo confronts us with his most profound question. Is it really true that this purely mundane conception of human knowledge leaves room for faith? The great void that religion seeks to fill—is it truly a positive sense of the absolute? Or is it merely a negative awareness that there is an extreme limit to research, and that we no longer can harbour the illusion that one day we may go beyond that limit?

Galileo found his answer in a sincere Christianity which he understood as an educative and moral force. His fight against Peripateticism was at one and the same time a fight for the liberation of man through truth and science and an apologia for a God very far removed from the God of the philosophers. His faith was serene and his science a liberation. As he opened the skies and built his instruments, he experienced a joy and a sense of strength and confidence. Because of this his proclamation of the truth addressed to all mankind in his extraordinary vernacular amounted, in his eyes, to a mission. Sagredo implored him in vain not to "put matters which can be demonstrated into circulation" and to leave the ignorant to their own fate: "If the preachers cannot convince obstinate sinners, why do you want to martyr yourself, to convert the ignorant? The ignorant, neither pre-destined nor elect, must be left to fall into the fire of their own ignorance." But Galileo replied: "Let truth be victorious!" The necessity to communicate is an integral part of the truth and so is the necessity to work for the good of all mankind. Here we witness the beginning, not the death throes of European science.

GALILEO THE PHILOSOPHER

¶ On May 7, 1610, Galileo wrote from Padua to Belisario Vinta. The letter is quoted often and contains an enumeration of all the projects that Galileo had in mind and wanted to carry out if the stipends offered by the Grand Duke of Tuscany would allow him to free himself of the burden of having to teach and afford him the leisure necessary for the realisation of his scientific plans. It is a very characteristic letter and bound to remind one of another no less famous one written by Leonardo da Vinci to the Duke of Milan. Galileo at that time was full of ideas and observations and at the height of his success. He had just given three lectures on the Medicean planets, to the great discomfiture of his enemies: "I am so full of special secrets, both useful and curious, which make one wonder; so much so that their mere abundance causes me pain . . ." For this reason he now wanted to co-ordinate his researches and produce a few works, which he listed—two of which were, in his eyes, of fundamental importance. "The works which I now must rapidly bring to a conclusion are mainly two books on the *system of the world or the constitution of the universe*. This is an enormous concept and full of philosophy, astronomy, and geometry. Then there are three books *De Motu Locali*, an entirely new science. Nobody else, neither ancient nor modern, has ever discovered any of the many marvellous symptoms which I will demonstrate to be present in both natural and forced motion. Hence I can very reasonably call it a new science developed by me from its first principles."[1]

The two ideas that described his conception of reality were, therefore, a system of the physical world and a general theory of motion. Under the latter term he also included the motion of animal bodies and he was planning, indeed, to write a treatise *De Animalium Motibus*. The all-inclusive concepts were motion, space, matter, and numbers. More than twenty years were to pass (and what years!) before the first of these intended works became in 1632 the *Dialogo . . . sopra i due massimi del mondo*. And only in 1638 his *De Motu Locali*, begun in Pisa almost half a century earlier, took shape as the *Discorsi e dimostrazioni matematiche intorno a due nove scienze attenenti alla meccanica ed ai movimenti locali*. This, at least, was the title improvised by the publisher, and not very acceptable to the author. This second book was published by the Elzevirs within a year of the *Discorsi* and several minor Cartesian works. The printer in his advertisement to the reader said: "In the present work . . . one sees that he was the discoverer of two entirely new sciences and of their basic principles and foundations demonstrated conclusively, that is geometrically. And . . . one of these sciences is about an eternal subject, of great importance in nature. It has been speculated upon by all the great philosophers, and many volumes have been written about it. I am speaking of motion . . . The other science too is demonstrated from its first principles. It deals with the resistance offered by solid bodies to being broken

---

[1] *Opere*, X, pp. 351–52.

by force. Its news is of great utility, especially in the mechanical arts and sciences . . . In this book the first doors are opened on these two new sciences both of which will make endless progress with the passage of time through the additions made to them by speculative intellects. And with a large number of demonstrated propositions one points to the progress and passage towards a further infinite number of doors."

In this text it is hardly necessary to underline the two ideas which came up again and again in the course of the sixteenth century. By now they had become almost commonplaces, something like fixed points in the intellectual climate of the age. The first idea concerns progress in the course of which there will be unravelled the conquests made by "speculative intellects." The motto "Truth is the daughter of time," which in 1536 had been used as a typographical decoration of the Venetian editions by Marcolino da Forlí,[2] stood with a new solemn meaning at the head of the 1611 Frankfurt edition of Kepler's *Narratio*, the book in which Kepler published his observations about the satellites of Jupiter. It was indeed a solemn opening, pregnant with meaning: "Who, if he is honest, will ever refuse to bear testimony to the truth? Which philosopher will ever hide the works of God? Who, unless he be more cruel than Pharaoh, will ever order the midwives to kill the newly born baby?" The identity of the new-born baby who was not to be killed, the truth to which one had to bear witness, had been revealed by Kepler the year before when he had published in Prague his *Dissertatio cum Nuncio Sidereo*. This truth concerned the worlds seen by Cusanus and Bruno. It concerned free philosophising—to use a term that (and this was no accident) came up again and again. "Free philoso-

---

[2] F. Saxl, "Veritas filia temporis," in: *Philosophy and History* (E. Cassirer Festschrift), New York, 1963, pp. 197–222.

phising, about the world and about nature," as Galileo put it.[3] It was, and here we come to the second of the two ideas, a "new science." The idea, so frequently mentioned in the later middle ages, that the world was aging and about to end in death was being replaced by the idea of rejuvenation, of a new age, of something new being brought about by the incessant march of time. We have had occasion to note how often, in the course of the sixteenth century, people had thought in terms of something *new:* new continents, new worlds, new stars, new sciences. After 1610, and not just once, one comes across, in letters written to Galileo, references to the necessary parallelism between the two most unsettling discoveries of the century—the continents of Columbus and the skies of Galileo. And with the new dimensions of the world, knowledge too had to be renewed. One had to affirm the need to look at physical reality in motion with instruments less sterile than those provided by Aristotelian logic.

There is a letter written by Fulgenzio Micanzio, dated from Venice, March 7, that is worth emphasising.[4] The writer recalls Paolo Sarpi "of glorious memory" and one of his favourite pronouncements, to the effect that "God and nature" had bestowed on Galileo the special gift of "understanding motion." It had not been an accident that the famous and decisive letter on the gravity of bodies of October 14, 1604, (from Padua) had been addressed to Sarpi. Friar Fulgenzio continued to speak of himself, of his dreams, and of the thoughts that filled his evenings. He was now always occupied with "the infinite, with indivisibility, and with the vacuum." Contrary to Aristotle, he had reached the conviction that without these things "there can be no motion and no operation

[3] *Opere*, III, I, p. 138ff.
[4] *Opere*, XVII, p. 42.

and, what is worse, no existence" and no life. He concluded with a highly significant observation: "It has occurred to me that in thinking about the book of nature, the characters of which are known to you alone . . . it is impossible that you should not also have given some thought to the kind of motion which we call voluntary and which is caused in our bodies by the mind." He was full of all sorts of obscure concepts about man. The new science of motion, consisting of clear concepts, was bound to invade the world of man, of voluntary motion, and of the imagination. Galileo himself wrote that if one is "searching for the seat of the vital faculties, tracing and observing the marvellous structures of the instruments which are the senses, one will never stop marvelling and never content oneself with the contemplation of the receptacles of the imagination, i.e. memory and speech."

Friar Fulgenzio's letter was written in March 1637. A few months later, in November, when twenty-three folios of the *Discorsi* had already been printed, Father Marin Mersenne sent to Galileo the *Discours de la méthode* which had just been published. He bemoaned the fact that the great Florentine philosopher, unlike Campanella, was not in Paris so that "we might be able to benefit in one and the same place by the two greatest men of the century." The good Father had published in 1634, in French, the then still unpublished treatise by Galileo on mechanics. He had added to it a preface of dithyrambic praise and an exhortation to the author to give to mankind the fruits of his solitary meditations, i.e. everything he knew about motion. Indeed, he added, "everything that comes from you will be excellent." The Roman condemnation had only just been pronounced. To Galileo's Parisian friends it signified the triumph of "ignorance, the mother of malignity, envy, and fury." "The time is now," Mersenne wrote. As he had done with the manuscript of *Le meccaniche*, he was to extract from the *Discorsi* very faithfully the French *Les Nouvelles Pensées de Galilée*. He was of the opinion that the "excellent mind of Mr. Galileo" was laying the foundations of a new way of understanding nature and was making a real science of it. He wrote in his compendium of *Les Méchaniques* that "nature cannot be cheated." "Nature is inexorable and without change and does not care whether its most recondite reasons and modes of operation are or are not exposed to the capacities of man (to understand) . . . and it never transgresses the limits of the laws imposed upon it." Nature never cheats and can never be cheated by machines. One cannot raise a weight with an instrument unless one employs a force equal to the one which would have been necessary if there had been no instrument. The new science, in proclaiming that "nature does not allow herself to be overcome or cheated by artfulness," pronounced a stern condemnation of all magico-alchemical fantasies and every belief in miracles. It made a clean sweep of the dream of the soul of the world and the souls of things. Nature was dominated by the mathematical rules of an honest game.[5] Galileo's words to this effect were being printed in Holland in 1637, the very year that Robert Fludd, the magician and theosophist against whom Kepler, Mersenne, and Gassendi had vindicated the significance of the new science, died. His numbers, his calculations, his mathematics, Kepler had written, are not mine. Nor were they those of Galileo, who in 1630 had read and appreciated Gassendi's attack on Fludd.

Father Mersenne understood fully everything that was new and rationally solid in the new science. And similarly he understood Galileo's "nature"—a nature that was inexorable, that could neither cheat nor be cheated but had to be measured rigorously and that

[5] *Opere*, II, pp. 115ff.

obeyed rational laws rigorously.[6] In his understanding of the reasoning by which, in different ways, his two great friends were exorcising the last of the malign and fraudulent spirits, the good Father was truly more saintly than the purveyors of the many equivocal fantasies of contemporary theology and philosophy. Galileo's physical researches laid the foundations of a new philosophy. As he discovered new provinces of the world, he directed his gaze deep into the constitution of things. In 1644, when he heard of Galileo's death, Mersenne wrote with much emotion: "He not only enlarged the provinces of the sky and increased the universe; he not only lit up the glassy orbs and the fragile stars, but also named the eternal bodies of the world in honour of the generosity of the Medici." These words are worth pondering. They express a contrast between the imaginary spheres and orbs, the fragile stars of "mathematical" hypotheses and the solidity of the eternal bodies of the world. Mersenne, faithful friend of Descartes though he was, had truly understood the whole import of Galileo's physics.

To tell the truth, it had not taken Galileo long to become aware of that import. If one turns from Mersenne's estimate to the letter addressed to Vinta in 1610, one will understand well its concluding remarks: "Finally, as far as my claims and titles are concerned, I would like to be known not only as a mathematician . . . but also as a philosopher. For I can claim to have studied philosophy for a greater number of years than the numbers of months I have spent on pure mathematics." There is no doubt that he was thinking of himself when he wrote to Pietro Dini in March 1615 a solemn eulogy of Copernicus,

---

[6] For all this see Mersenne, *Correspondence*, edited by Mme. Paul Tannery-Cornelis de Waard, Vols. II and III, Paris, 1945ff.; also R. Lenoble, *Mersenne et la naissance du mécanisme*, Paris, 1943.

a eulogy that was very similar to the one written by Bruno: "And then, donning the gown of a philosopher, he considered whether such a constitution of the parts of the universe could really subsist in the nature of things. He saw that it could not; nevertheless, it seemed to him that the problem of the true constitution was worth probing, and he dedicated himself to its investigation. He recognised that even though a disposition of parts that is imaginary and not true can satisfy appearances, a real truth would be much more satisfactory. And one would gain in philosophy an excellent knowledge, that is, the knowledge of the true disposition of the parts of the world."

Galileo's proud but significant claim to be a philosopher was not an isolated whim, nor was it conditioned by the demands of his reputation. In claiming for himself the title of philosopher he expressed a very clear intention. He was thinking of something other than a mere increase in salary or a qualification more respected in academic circles. In the August of 1612 he was still talking about it in a spirited fashion to the faithful and open-minded Sagredo, his intelligent and unprejudiced partner in conversation. On August 12 Sagredo replied as follows: "If I have drawn in the letters I have written to you a distinction between philosophers and mathematicians—and it seems that you have heard a rumour of my distinction—I would like you to know that I have used this distinction in conformity with common usage. According to common usage philosophers are people who know nothing about natural things and are indeed incapable of understanding them. They nevertheless pretend to be privy to nature's plans. And with that reputation they try to stupefy the senses of man and to deprive them of the use of reasons."[7]

These words of Sagredo's make one think: they express without reticence the widely held belief that

---

[7] *Opere*, XI, p. 379.

people were equally bored by the Platonising rhetoric that had been so fashionable in the fifteenth century and by scholastic Peripateticism, tied up in knots as it had been for nearly two centuries and lost in blind alleys. This Peripateticism was sterile and petulant, and some people with involuntary irony are wont to call its upholders the "precursors of Galileo." It was not only that the endless fifteenth-century debates about the intellect had not managed to break new ground, but also that the researches into the problem of motion had remained surrounded by logical subtleties that had failed to transcend the limits imposed by custom and by the boring game known as *ad utramque partem* that so annoyed Galileo, "used as he was," and he repeated this with eloquence, "to study in the book of nature . . . in the open book of the sky . . . where things are written in one way only." For that matter, he was also accustomed to study in "the books that contained demonstrations, i.e. mathematics, not those written by logicians." Galileo's and Sagredo's rebellions were not isolated ones. On August 23, 1612, Luca Valerio took the field in defence of "free philosophising which is not bound by the rules of a certain philosophical grammar or a grammatical philosophy." In July 1613 Orazio Morandi proclaimed that there was only one truth and that it was open only to those who are "enrolled under her victorious banners." It can be grasped by those who "philosophise by contemplating the beautiful and ample book of nature and are not tied down by the sophisms of people who want not only to incarcerate that unhappy science but also to push it into the deepest dungeons of Aristotelian opinion and hand it over to the caprices of those philosophers who *iudicant in verba insani magistri.*"

It was in this environment that Galileo's assumption of the name philosopher acquired its precise meaning. It was not a question of obtaining a more important university chair—that of natural philosophy

or physics, which would have given its occupant a
position of greater importance than one in mathematics or astronomy. It was rather a question of a plain
rejection of the antics of the logicians, of a plain affirmation that the new cosmological doctrines were
real and not hypothetical. What mattered was the
awareness that the vision of the physical universe
revealed by experience and by mathematical demonstrations was complete and exhaustive—at least in
that sphere of knowledge which was capable of rational justification. Beyond that sphere there was only
faith, and that was an altogether different matter. The
telescope and the magnet, correctly used as mathe-
matico-logical instruments, the phases of Venus and
the solar spots, heliocentrism and the laws of motion
—all these, though they were not intended to touch
upon the religious validity of Christianity, combined
to destroy without respite the Aristotelian picture
of reality with its hopeless confusion of physics and
metaphysics. The new conception by contrast aimed
to include the whole world of animal motion and of
the psychic activities of man. It was no accident that
the ordinary curriculum in philosophy consisted of a
commentary on the books of *De Anima* as well as of
a commentary on the books on physics and the heavens. Galileo's appeal to another text led to the study
of the same chapter headings, with the book of nature substituted for the books of Aristotle. In his
writings, in his letters, and even in his conversations
such as have come down to us, there is reference again
and again to the ancient *topos* of the book. This was
not only because the *topos* was commonly used but
because Galileo pursued a polemical end with it. One
had to learn and teach, he was saying, no longer with
the help of Aristotle's book but through an autonomous elaboration of knowledge. Today we would put
it that one had to learn by going to the things themselves, using adequate instruments such as sensations
and concepts, experiences and demonstrations suitably

integrated with one another. This all meant that one no longer "had to adapt nature and the world to Peripatetic doctrine, . . . but philosophy to the world and to nature." We must no longer "in the company of timid and servile intellects" limit ourselves "to the interpretation of the sayings of other men just because we happen to be men, letting our eyes gaze day and night upon pictures printed on paper without ever raising them to what is true and real, what is made by God with His own hands. For it is this latter book which, for our instruction, is always open in front of us."

It was probably prudence which recommended a certain silence about authors who shared his ideas. There may even have been a somewhat ostentatious refusal to acknowledge the existence of contemporary works by other "free philosophers." In the last analysis Galileo's purpose was to aim at grasping reality in a different manner. In more cases than one he was by no means averse to taking cognisance of what other people were saying. But when he did take notice, it was always on condition that these sayings remain a means for coming into direct contact with things. Someone else can help us to recover reality; but ultimately we must discover reality personally, with our own eyes, not through the eyes of someone else. For this reason, as Viviani recorded, "it seemed to him that . . . the freedom of the countryside was the book of nature, which was always open to him who enjoyed reading and studying it with his own eyes." And for this reason, Gherardini remarked, "he owned very few books and his researches depended upon continuous observation in that he deduced a philosophical argument from everything he saw, heard, or touched." That much was expressed by Galileo himself in a fine passage: "In natural matters, man's authority is of no value . . . Nature . . . makes fun of the constitutions and decrees of princes, emperors, and monarchs. She would not alter an iota

of her laws and statutes at their request. Aristotle was
a man. He saw with his eyes, heard with his ears,
spoke through his brain. I am a man. I see with my
eyes, and more than he did. As far as talking is
concerned, I believe he talked about more things
than I am wont to talk about. But whether he spoke
as well as I do in those things that we both have
spoken about depends on the reasons we advance: not
on our authorities. Such a great man, you will say,
who has had so many followers? This counts for
nothing, for the number of his adherents is due to
his antiquity and to the number of years that have
passed. One cannot conclude that a father who is
seventy years old and has twenty sons is more fertile
than one of his young sons who so far has one son
only and is only twenty years old." He kept hammer-
ing at this point and one must not allow the primary
intention to escape. His insistence on it was polemical. He attacked a reigning doctrine and the prevalent
method of teaching—for Galileo was always linked
to the schools, and it was against the schools that he
rebelled. One must take these polemics into account
without however giving too much way to the temptation to make explicit, not even with gentle forcing,
what is merely implied in his preference for seeing
and reading, and for the telescope. Above everything
there was the importance of the doctrines of the
two books in which God was revealed: nature and the
Bible. It is true that Galileo himself was fond of
metaphors rich in metaphysical implications. And at
times these metaphors were expanded into forms characteristic of Platonic doctrines. When he had to provide a theoretical justification for the heliocentric
system he did so in terms that came close to heliolatry
and to the metaphysics of light. In his letter to Pietro
Dini of March 24, 1614, there are whole passages
that could have been penned by a Platonist two centuries earlier. Referring to Psalm XVIII he wrote a
page which is unforgettable: "I would say that it

seems to me that there is in nature a substance that is utterly spiritual, constant, and fast moving. It is diffused throughout the universe and penetrates into everything without distinction. It heats, vivifies, and fertilises all living persons. Sense itself demonstrates that the body of the sun is the principal receptacle of that spirit. From that receptacle there expands throughout the universe an immense light, which is accompanied by great heat, and which penetrates into all vegetable bodies and makes them alive and fertile. One can reasonably assess that this spirit is something more than light, for it penetrates into all bodily substances, no matter how thick they are . . . Hence we can affirm with great likelihood that this fertile spirit and this light diffused throughout the universe come together, and are united in the solar body because it is situated in the centre of the universe. From there, made even more splendid and vigorous, it diffuses itself again." Galileo then continued to explain that the first-born light, which is the spirit itself, *fovens aquas*, is all gathered in the sun and explodes as the animating power of the cosmos. "It is very likely that in the heart of animals there is a continuous regeneration of vital spirits which sustain and vivify all the members of the animal's body. The spirit also comes into the heart, ministering food and giving the nourishment without which the animal would perish. Even so in the sun, while something comes into it from the outside, there is also conserved the spring from which there is continuously derived and diffused that light and prolific heat which gives life to all the members which are seated around it."[8]

---

[8] It is useful to compare Antonio Perseo, *Trattato dell'ingegno dell'huomo*, Venice, 1576, p. 126f. But cp. Tullio Gregory, "Studi sull'atomismo del Seicento, I, Sebastiano Basson," *Giornale critico della filosofia italiana*, 43, 1964, pp. 38–65. P. Wiener, "The Tradition behind Galileo's Methodology," *Osiris*, I, 1936, pp. 733–46, is a curious example of an

Ricasoli Rucellai, in his dialogue *Ad Anazimandrum*, found in texts like these a theory of the soul of the world and other echoes of Ficino. It was no accident that Galileo was leaning on the Pseudo-Dionysius. Sources and parallelisms can be found without difficulty. There was a Pythagorean, a Hermetic, and a Neoplatonic intuition. There was the cult of the sun, so dear to Giuliano, and which had been the presupposition and basis, explicit and clear, of the Copernican hypothesis. All this can be found too often in Galileo's writings to be accidental. It clearly demonstrates how difficult it is to distinguish, as Koyré, in a passage quoted above, wanted to do, between mystical and geometrical Platonism, or between Plotinus, Proclus, and Ficino on one side and Euclid and Archimedes on the other.

To say this is to say no more than that Galileo was breathing the air of a certain cultural climate. It does not prove that his philosophy was a form of Platonism and even less that it was a Platonism of Ficino's variety. For that matter, the fact that he occasionally expressed an Aristotelian judgment (e.g. the letter to Liceti of September 15, 1640) does not mean that he, implacable foe of Peripateticism that he was, had any liking for Aristotle. There are two things, rather, which one ought to remember. First,

_____

insufficient historical analysis. Its main argument is as follows: "I wish to show that Galileo's methodology was opposed not to the intellectual traditions of Greek thought but to a specious Aristotelianism current in his day: that wherever Galileo diverged from Aristotle, it was not in method but in content; finally, that the innovations in the contents of his physical doctrines were made by Galileo within the framework of a Platonic conception of the physical world." There is hardly any support for any of these views. Wiener's vague approximation to the facts of history result from the way in which he leans on Sizzi and on his *Dianonia* as if it were completely Peripatetic.

his heliocentrism was part, at least to begin with, of a general vision which took its inspiration from the sun—a vision which had both preceded and accompanied the Copernican revolution and which had charged it with speculative implications that went far beyond the mere upheaval of an old astronomical theory. Second, at the very moment that Galileo, with his physical theories, lent his hand to the fashioning of a new conception of the world, he was compelled to defend himself against many different accusations and therefore to seek the support of all kinds of doctrines that happened to be in circulation and possessed some kind of authority. On the metaphysical side, there was Platonism, or better, the composite body of doctrines that had been the presupposition of Copernicanism. They had been taken up by Bruno and had affected Kepler whose complex and involved problems it is not easy to dissect.

We have thus reached a question that has often been discussed, but rarely in exact terms. It is the question of the relationship between Galileo and the currents of sixteenth-century thought, be it those of Platonism or those of the Aristotelianism of the schools or those of the rebellious and reforming views of Telesio, Cardano, Bruno, Della Porta, and Campanella. There is another question connected with it, i.e. the question of the so-called precursors of Galileo. By "precursors" one usually means not the one man who was at least in part worthy of that name, Leonardo da Vinci, but the late medieval physicists and their hopeless sixteenth-century imitators.

Plato's impetuous return, which had changed the whole non-academic culture of the fifteenth century, had adapted itself sufficiently easily to something like a peaceful coexistence with Peripateticism. The program for this coexistence had been outlined by Ficino, that great mediator. According to this program, Aristotle had remained the teacher of logic and physics; and Plato, interpreted through Plotinus and Proclus, had found his place between theology and metaphysics. If one looks at the philosophical lessons taught in Italian universities throughout the century, one will, in more than one case, gain the impression that this division into separate fields was accepted quietly, even though there were the odd border clashes. In one way or another the ancient commentators, Temistius, Simplicius, Alexander, and Philoponus, were adapted to this system. In the case of Alexander of Aphrodisia there were some real difficulties; and on the whole Simplicius gained some pre-eminence. The whole of metaphysics came to be full of combinations, concords, symphonies, and such like, and there was a general atmosphere of Platonisation which affected, no matter how lightly, even that most ardent of men, Bruno. But of greater importance, perhaps, is the example of a man more closely linked with Galileo. There taught in Padua, during the last third of the century, the crypto-Platonist Francesco Piccolomini, who called Plato the other eye of the soul. He inspired and perhaps even wrote works for young Venetian patricians such as Pietro Duedo who, in 1609, was *riformatore dello studio*. On the other side, in Pisa, between 1588 and 1597, Jacopo Mazzoni lectured on Aristotle. But Mazzoni also gave extra-curricular lectures on Plato. He was both a teacher of and a friend to Galileo. In appearance he was a concordist, but in substance a Platonist. And it was he, with his *De Comparatione Aristotelis et Platonis*, who provoked Galileo's first frank defence, expressed in the latter's letter of May 30, 1597, from Padua, stating that he was of the "opinion of Pythagoras and Copernicus about the motion and the place of the earth."[9] But there was more. Referring to a letter by Mazzoni, Galileo sent to Kepler on August 4 a profession of faith in Copernicus and called Copernicanism the only method of philosophy which is not

---

[9] *Opere*, II, pp. 197–202.

perverse. This profession was made all the more gladly because he had "accepted the theory of Copernicus for many years and found at its bottom also the causes of a great many natural effects, inexplicable on the basis of traditional theory." He added: "I have written many demonstrations and refutations of the arguments which have been advanced against it, but frightened by the fate of Copernicus, our common teacher, I have not dared to publish them."

In fact, we possess only the rejoinder to Mazzoni. It is worth dwelling on his links with Galileo. In 1590, when Galileo was teaching mathematics in Pisa, he wrote to his father that he was planning to "study under and learn from Mr. Mazzoni." In 1597, when he had finished reading the *Comparatio*, he wrote immediately about it: "To me in particular it has given the greatest satisfaction and comfort . . . to see you on some of those questions we used to discuss so gaily taking the side which I had considered true but which you then had considered to be false." The echoes of these debates are indeed very evident not only in those many pages in which Mazzoni deals with up and down motion, but also in those in which he confronts Aristotle with the Platonists' use of mathematical devices in physics: "Plato believed that mathematics was most suited to physical researches and he availed himself of it to uncover physical mysteries." But there is more. Basing himself on a text from Proclus, Mazzoni managed to formulate some kind of a synthesis between Democritus and the *Timaeos*. He wrote as follows: "Proclus argues that Plato assumed that before the four elements were quantitatively differentiated, there existed regular corpuscles. And thus he demonstrated that heat and cold depend on the degree of obtuseness of their angles." He concluded that it was by no means an error into which Plato had fallen through his love of mathematics, but that it had been a supreme stroke of shrewdness that had made him see and reach the cause of heat and cold. This is only Galileo's well-known theory about primary and secondary qualities in a nutshell.[10] He could have continued speaking not so much of the use to which Archimedes was being put and of the habits of medieval opticians, but of those parts of Benedetti's work of 1685 which were not mentioned explicitly by Galileo but which had been analysed by him with explicit reference to Mazzoni. There is no doubt that in some parts it reflects the "gay and friendly" debates in Pisa. It is of interest to add that in 1597 there was yet another text of natural philosophy in which Francesco Piccolomini was quoted. Piccolomini was at that time a colleague of Galileo in Padua. In the text quoted he discusses the Aristotelian theories about the gravity of bodies in the light of the criticism of "several mathematicians." We seek in vain for anything similar in the *Quaestiones Naturales* of his opponent, the much younger but already deceased Jacopo Zabarella —a much more astute thinker and a coherent Aristotelian. In fact, during the last two decades of the century, Peripateticism was singularly conservative in those spheres in which it had remained dominant, that is in logic and natural philosophy. So much so that it had become completely lost in a blind alley.

In the fifteenth century there had been a rebirth of Platonism. The texts of classical natural science had become more conspicuous, and commentaries on Aristotle never or hardly ever used had come to the fore. This had led to repercussions not only in metaphysics, morals, politics, and aesthetics but also in questions of method, in psychology, and in the sciences of life. As was to be expected, the storm broke loose, already at the beginning of the century, in the

---

[10] J. Mazzoni, *In universam Platonis et Aristotelis philosophiam praeludia*, Venice, 1957, pp. 189ff. For the corpuscular theories attributed to Plato see the texts by Basson, quoted by Gregory, *op. cit.*, p. 51.

border regions. To be precise it had affected first, in the region where psychology bordered on metaphysics, the question of the immortality of the soul. And in the region where logic bordered on metaphysics it had affected the problem of the classification of the sciences, or the problem of the systematisation of knowledge. By the end of the century these outbursts tended to die down and calm returned to the problem of method and to natural philosophy. It was then that the rebirth caused a real explosion, this time not within the orbit of the Peripateticism which had survived, but outside it. It led to bitter clashes between mathematicians, opticians, and physicians and such like. These clashes were nourished and encouraged by non-Aristotelian and anti-Aristotelian currents. Too many historians have fallen into the error of seeking a continuity between medieval debates and the new original standpoints. It is undeniable that the former had contributed something towards the corrosion of Aristotelianism, without really succeeding. But it is equally true that the latter were based upon experiences, and that these, in turn, had been made possible by new instruments and even more so by a completely different set of preferences. Galileo, in his *De Motu*, though still tied to the theories of impetus, wrote that Aristotle had been opposed to the ancients and that we were for the ancients. Galileo systematically sided with the ancients, whose opinions had been destroyed by Aristotle without cause. He considered Archimedes "divine" and thought that his intellect was superior to any other. In a famous passage of the *Dialogo* he expressed his unreserved admiration for Aristarchos and Copernicus because they had used their reason to violate their senses, so much so that "reason had finally mastered their credulity." With all this Galileo shows that he had made a complete break with the conceptions in traditional physics and logic which continued to be favoured by Aristotelianism. Without that subversion and without new general

theories there would have been no point in putting
the eye to the telescope. The spots of the sun even
when observed would have continued to cheat the
senses. The new techniques, the crafts of the artisan,
of the building yards and the arsenals, would have
remained silent, isolated from scientific research and
without communication with the world of scientists.

This break, this mental revolution, this change in
the co-ordinates of knowledge, was not caused in
Galileo by a further deepening of the theories of
impetus or by a more profound understanding of
the debates on *intensio et remissio formarum*. It was
caused by his sudden grasp of the fact that Copernicus' heroic vision was not a mathematical hypothesis but a real vision of things, i.e. that it was to be
taken in Bruno's sense. Copernicus' vision had had
a profound effect on Galileo and forced him away
not only from the last residues of Aristotelian physics
but also from the general theoretical presuppositions
that that physics had implied. Copernicus' theory was
for him a philosophy fashioned not only outside the
limits of Peripateticism but also outside the limits of
all attempts at compromises, for compromises only
too often unconsciously ended up with the acceptance of equivocal promises and were bound to suffer
the consequences of that equivocation. In 1610 Kepler
wrote with good reason that behind the *Sidereus
Nuncius* there stood Cusanus and Bruno and an
entire conception of the universe which, in spite
of the fact that it invoked Pythagoras and Melissus
and Democritus and Plato, amounted to a total revolution of all thought about the relationship between man
and the world. It was a conception which had forced
an entirely new manner of research upon us. Copernicanism, understood as a conception of the universe
and not simply as a mathematical theory, was a revolutionary vision, and as such it was the fruit of the
first attempts at theory made in the early Renaissance.
One could look upon it as the realisation of certain

possibilities implied in the so-called Platonism of Cusanus and Ficino. One need only look at the opening lines of Copernicus' work (1, 12) in order to see this. Bruno had understood it thus, and thus it was understood by Galileo when he wrote in 1597 to Kepler that he had been able to understand the problem of motion only on the basis of Copernicus' theory. It is a passage which had made people think, for how indeed could Galileo at that time have demonstrated the Copernican theories? The truth is that he had found in them a starting point, a new basis, a new intuition. They presented him with another way of seeing the world, one that was freed of all Aristotelian equivocations. At last he was able to see the world and to examine its problems with new eyes.

Copernicanism was a philosophy. It was a philosophy insofar as it was a presupposition. But it was a presupposition in a sense very different from the one in which it had been used in the Platonising circles of the Renaissance, and by the Archimedean Platonism mentioned by Koyré. In 1597 Galileo had taken a different point of departure. When he progressed from the study of the laws of motion, conducted in an increasingly original sense, to the study of the heavens, his Copernicanism became transformed. There came a moment at which the *Sidereus Nuncius* demolished the structure of the Aristotelian world. This demolition was carried out not by a metaphysical and practical vision of nature as in Bruno, but with the help of mathematical demonstrations and of sense experience refined by instruments. With this demolition Galileo's philosophy of nature completely changed its character. Once the barriers of the sky were down and the hierarchical and finalistic conceptions abandoned, the physical world unified and the logico-cognitive processes clarified, Galileo's Copernicanism assumed new dimensions. Having become natural, i.e. scientific, the knowledge of the sky as well as of the earth and of all relationships changed

and with them the limits of the realm of man. With
the sky, the stars, and space subject to the new realm
of a unified science that was ready to specify the
laws of every possible field of experience, all ultimate
problems began to appear in a new light: would it
really be possible for that experience and that knowledge to combine in order to embrace in one fell
swoop the infinite, the absolute, the All? With this
question the paths separated. Giordano Bruno would
have replied in the affirmative. Galileo was to reply in
the negative. In spite of certain similarities of expression with which the two thinkers refer to the
relationship between science and faith, between the
realm of man and the realm of God, the differences
remain extremely great. Hence Galileo's silence in
regard to Bruno's case was justified, apart from mere
considerations of prudence. Galileo's philosophy was
a science, i.e. the fruit of experience and reason. It
was plainly valid in a sphere that was destined to
become enlarged as time went by. There were no
barriers; but it was limited to dimensions other than
those of the absolute and the divine. It was a science
which did not seek ultimate essences. As a science, it
knew nothing of the absolute infinite, and as science
it did not express an opinion on it. For this reason
it could never come into conflict with the pronouncements of faith, which had other instruments,
other objects, another book. But for the philosopher
there was only one book of reason and nature, of
mathematics and experience, based on the reality that
is seen with the eyes, and of which the mind is able
to think on the basis of information supplied by the
senses, perfected by instruments and helped by log-
ico-rational calculations. The book of philosophy is a
book of this world, containing the guarantees and
measures in which action and knowledge overlap
and intersect, in which knowledge without action
is sterile. The break with Aristotle occurred at the
point at which Galileo denied that there was an

absolute contrast between types of motion, between heaven and earth, between what is corruptible and what is incorruptible, between nature and super-nature. Human nature is unified in its spatial texture and becomes measurable in the rhythm of time and the grooves of its laws. The kingdom of God is altogether different, and access to it is by different means. Its book is of a different kind.

The new philosophy was no longer an intuited presupposition but a verified theory. As such it detached itself from primitive Copernicanism. After 1610 this new philosophy became the focal point of Galileo's reflections and experimentation. His so-called propaganda is nothing less than a general doctrine whose importance is much greater than any one single discovery he ever made. This doctrine amounts to a new way of understanding philosophy as a human search and a human construction. It is something for men, something which takes place in the realm in which men live. It is aware of the limits imposed upon that realm and conscious of other possible dimensions. In its own field, however, it is autonomous and a measure unto itself.

Hence the distance which separates Galileo from Descartes, as well as from Bruno. This distance is due to the fact that Galileo was clearly aware of the limits of all philosophical thinking and did not wish to return to the equivocations of Peripateticism with its lugubrious marriage of physics to metaphysics. But the distance also has something to do with Galileo's heroic determination to proclaim the truth. He was set upon making the truth available to everybody, upon publishing it and seeking verification in collaboration with others, in a common liberation from errors. Galileo could not continue his work under a mask.

This interpretation of his thought seems confirmed by the path along which his reflections gradually became defined. He was a student of medicine in 1581.

As late as 1590 he still recalled his Galen. We know from the lecture notes of Pisan students of these years that great importance was then attached to questions of logic and method, and from the teachings of Cesalpino, Mercuriale, and Liceti we know how complex the problems of the sciences of life were.[11]

Galileo's notes from the year 1584 are well known. They are a precious document of his Aristotelian point of departure in questions about the heavens, the "intension and remission of forms," and the qualities. These pieces, written in his own hand, reflect his thorough knowledge of the scholastic explanations current in Pisa. This is proved, for example, by his quotations from the lectures of Flaminio Nobili. Following Favaro's reasoning, it is widely accepted that the lectures in question were by Francesco Buonamici. However a comparison with the monumental *De Motu* by the Pisan teacher, published in Florence in 1591, reveals only very partial correspondences in the arguments of the tenth book. In addition to this there are many notable differences in the tone of the quotations and the manner of speech. And in Galileo's *Juvenilia* there is a complete absence of the strong attacks on the Platonic theories concerning the corruptibility of the heavens and the usefulness of mathematics. But there is more. Buonamici remarked that he had arrived at the conception of his work through the recent discussions about motion that had taken place at the university of Pisa between members of his audience and his colleagues. This was in 1591. The oldest writings by Galileo on motion date from 1590. And we would do well to pay attention to his observations and his discussions with Mazzoni. These are most critical and very detached from the atmosphere that the work of Buonamici breathes.

---

11 Cp. J. Roger, *Les sciences de la vie dans la pensée française du XVIII*, Paris, 1963. The long introduction contains a description of European research of the sixteenth century.

Therefore we ought to examine Galileo's *Juvenilia* on physics, and the notes on logic, also in his own writing. All the notes have the same origin and none of them were used by Favaro. Here we find discussions about the relative importance of the sciences and on their principles and their order. These discussions are similar to the ones we find for instance in the logical maxims of Zabarella of the second half of the sixteenth century. The questions Galileo raised are much more important than the trite formulae about resolution and composition, but Randall has tried to see them as proof that Galileo's method was all of a piece with the Peripateticism of the schools. A collection of all the *Juvenilia* will also help us to form an idea of the earliest cultural experiences of Galileo and to question the alleged links with Buonamici. At the very time when Buonamici wrote his *De Motu*, Galileo was about to embark on a different course, which was destined to lead him outside that cosmic order and that notion of space in which the Pisan master had firmly planted his bodies, both heavy and light. As Galileo remarked, he had done so for no other reason than that they had to be found in *some* order.

The destruction of that order, the influence of Archimedes, the denial that there were heavy bodies and light bodies, the transformation of the concept of space, the beginning of the thought process which was to lead to the refutation of the idea that the world had a centre, and towards a notion of relativity—all these stemmed from Galileo's interpretation of Copernicanism as a vision of reality rather than as a mathematical hypothesis. It is of special importance that he confessed to Kepler in 1597 that he had used Copernicus' theories for years as the foundation of his study of the laws of motion. His observations were to confirm his idea that objective reality corresponded to the proportions expressed by numbers. And finally there came the telescope, an extension of the senses analogous to the extension of reason through mathematics. It allowed him to see that the *true* sky is very different from the sky of Peripateticism, that the world *is* indeed different. In this way the experience of the senses proved that Copernicus' world was true. We have quite a few documents which illustrate Galileo's attitude. There is for instance his reply to Cesi, who had raised some judicious doubts in regard to the Copernican concessions about epicycles and eccentricity: "We must not demand that nature accommodate herself to what seems more sensible to us; instead, we ought to accommodate our intellect to what nature has done." Philosophy must stop being a "chimera of our brain," as Gallanzoni was to put it. The telescope—i.e. our eyes' increased power—and mathematics—i.e. our mind refined for deeper understanding—allow us access to a reality which corresponds to them and which is objectively measurable. It is true that we do not find in Galileo a search for the justification of such measurability. There is nothing in Galileo like the Cartesian doctrine about the veracity of God apart from the famous pages of the *Dialogo* about intensive and extensive knowledge. But there is no Pythagorean-Platonic development of the idea that the cosmos has a mathematical structure. There is no more than the many well-known references to Plato throughout his works. The truth is that Galileo was neither writing about logic nor composing a treatise on method: he was searching for the rules of how to swim by jumping into the water and swimming. He used Copernicus as a springboard. But the sinews of his whole philosophy consisted in his systematic elimination of physico-theological equivocations, in the precise demarkation of the field of scientific knowledge, in his claim that the whole of the world of experiences must be subject to rational investigation, and in his focus upon the mutual integration of mathematics with sense experience. Primarily he aimed at the construction of a physics independent of both pseudo-philosophical and pseudo-theological theories.

His attitude towards religion was made more and more precise as his support of Copernicus came to be better and better verified. There was no doubt as to the sincerity of his faith. But at the same time there was no doubt as to his complete conviction that religion belongs to another sphere and that it cannot interfere with the world which is subject to reason and which belongs to science. His quarrel with the Peripatetics as well as his estrangement from his own contemporaries, including Kepler, had its roots in the need to liberate scientific knowledge from concepts which belonged to other orders, and from the interference of institutions which were opposed to it. On the other hand he had a deep respect for the supernatural as such. The expulsion of Aristotelianism however meant that one had to stop looking for the reflection of the divine in the crystalline purity of the moon. God, if He is the root of everything, is also beyond everything. For this reason, the science that refused to seek the infinite in any one particular act was also the science that restored to the infinite its real and transcendental majesty.

It is fashionable nowadays to quote the famous play by Brecht. In one of his most eloquent passages, Brecht made Friar Fulgenzio confess to the master that he did not have the courage to tell his parents, worn out by a life without pleasures, that there is no intelligible benign and just God watching them from beyond the beams of their ceiling.

Galileo's philosophy—and philosophy with Galileo—does not place God within the orbit of its own reasoning. It has no place for Him as a Person among other persons, on the stage of the world. It destroys a homely image of the universe and places God at a distance which cannot be measured in human terms. In spite of all this, Galileo continued to feel he was Christian, a member of his church and a defender of the human and moral meaning of his faith against all pseudo-philosophical mystification. But quite literally, the kingdom of God is not of this world. If the old, homely images of the universe have their uses in the education of mankind they have nothing to do with philosophy. There is a moment at which science has to assert itself against the clamour of the market-place, as Leonardo had put it. At that point, truth imposes silence upon its false priests who parade as philosophers. Reason then understands its own limitations and becomes aware of the true meaning of faith. The tasks of reason are precisely set out and reason does not hold out the illusory hope to man that there are final explanations. Faith, on the other hand, is the ultimate meaning of the universe. Thus the human situation is less comforting and less peaceful, and reflection affords little consolation. The spring of faith, however, is indissolubly linked with the incomprehensibility of life, with its inevitable tragedy. This faith and its God are justified in the realm of the practical and thus, at the very birth of modern thought, Galileo reminds one more of Pascal than of Descartes.

MAGIC AND ASTROLOGY
IN THE CIVILISATION
OF THE RENAISSANCE

(Thomas Campanella, in his *The Meaning of Things and of Magic*, wrote as follows:

Everything done by scientists in imitation of nature or to help nature through unknown artifices is regarded not only by the vulgar crowds but also by all men in general as the working of magic. In this way not only the said sciences but all others as well are taken to serve the purposes of magic. It was considered magic when Archita made a dove which could fly like a natural one. And at the time of the Emperor Ferdinand in Germany, a German constructed an artificial eagle and a fly which flew by themselves. But since the art was not understood, all this was called magic. Later, all this became ordinary science.

The invention of gunpowder for the harquebus, of printing, and of the loadstone were taken to be due to magic. But today everybody knows how these things are made. People have lost their reverence for the making of clocks and for the other mechanical arts, for their methods have become obvious to everybody. But matters of physics, astrology, and religion are rarely understood. Hence the ancients used to reserve the term "magic" for these arts.[1]

With much acumen, Campanella emphasised three points. First, all sciences, insofar as they inquire into the structure of reality, are subservient to magic, for magic is a practical activity which aims at the transformation of nature by interfering with the laws of nature through technical knowledge of how they operate. Secondly, the mysterious aura which used to surround every magician as if he were a god had been diminished with the progress of science. Thirdly, it is nevertheless true that the highest problems and therefore the most profound questions, are incapable of rational comprehension and remain therefore covered by the mysterious veil of magic.

Thus we are on the road to a new appreciation of magic and astrology, the inseparable companion of magic. Among human activities, the working of magic assumes a central position, for in magic one finds an almost exemplary expression of the divine power in man which Campanella celebrated in verses that have become rightly famous. The man in the centre of the universe is precisely the man who has comprehended the secret rhythm of nature and who thus becomes a poet. He is the man who, like a God, does not confine himself to writing words in ink on mere pieces of

---

[1] IV, 5, Bruers, ed., Bari, 1925, pp. 241–42. The following general works are of fundamental importance to the subject: *Catalogus codicum astrologorum Graecorum*, Brussels, 1898ff., 18 vols. Ptolemaeus, *Tetrabiblos*, Leipzig, ed. Boll-Boer, 1940; Vettius Valens, *Anthologiarum libri*, Berolini, ed. Kroll, 1908; Bouché-Leclerq, *Astrologie grecque*, Paris, 1899; Boll-Bezold, *Sternglaube und Sterndeutung*, IV ed. by W. Gundel, Leipzig, 1931; Boll, *Sphaera*, Leipzig, 1903; Lynn Thorndike, *A History of Magic and Experimental Science*, 6 vols., New York, 1923ff.; W. E. Peuckert, *Pansophie*, Stuttgart, 1936; A. J. Festugière, *La révélation d'Hermès Trismégiste*, I, *L'astrologie et les sciences occultes*, Paris, 1950.

paper but imprints real things upon the grand and living book of the world.

In order to understand adequately the problem of magic as it appeared at the dawn of modern civilisation, one must above all remember that with the coming of the Renaissance it emerged from the subterranean regions to which it had been confined during the middle ages, into the full light of day. In the middle ages magic had been widely known and practised, but with the coming of modern thought, it assumed a new garb and began to occupy the minds of all great scientists and thinkers. Although in their minds it became somewhat purified, it remained of great importance. This is true even for those—and I might say, especially for those—who, like Leonardo, inveighed bitterly against the inept practitioners of necromantic cults. If we confine ourselves to the major thinkers, we find that Marsilio Ficino devoted a considerable proportion of his writings on life to magic. Giovanni Pico della Mirandola wrote a fervent and courageous apology for magic. Giordano Bruno defined the magician as a wise man who has the power to act. And the same Bruno in his *Theses de Magia*, his attempt to determine according to an ancient system the hierarchy of beings and of the powers exercised by God on things, emphasised the two movements that run through the whole of the scale. Among these movements there is above all the magic action which rises towards the heavens and joins things together, brings those which are opposed into harmony, composes all earthly struggles, causes all elements to form one sublime consonance. Of all things he held that magic, by working miracles, would enter into the hearts of men through spells and incantations and thus bring about a radical reformation of the earthly city.

Francis Bacon owed a great deal to the teachings of alchemy and magic when he insisted that science was power, and that scientific knowledge is a form of activity which listens to the language of nature in order to dominate her, issues commands to her, and transforms her into a useful servant. Kepler believed that the spheres of the heavens were moved by spirits and took exception to Pico's criticism of astrology.[2] Leibniz, following Lullus and Bruno, pursued cabbalistic mysteries in order to find the key to the logic that was to unravel all secrets. Even the cold and rigorous mind of Descartes showed traces of these preoccupations. As a young man he had been inspired by the writings of Cornelius Agrippa of Nettelsheim to give substance to the dream of an *ars magna* and had sought to grasp the *fundamentum mirabile* of knowledge in Lullus' calculations. But even when he renounced all these bad books and bad arts, he did not abandon the attempt to find the secrets of life and the method for prolonging life and overcoming death by examining corpses.

Agrippa and Paracelsus, Cardano and Della Porta and many others, some well known and others not so well known, all followed Campanella's program to reduce magic to science. It is important not to misunderstand this reduction. One must not look upon it merely as an attempt to absorb those calculations which the scheme of traditional logic had confined to the periphery or as an attempt to purify magic of its turgid appeal to obscure demonic forces. The reduction should not be seen as a linear progression in which the manner of seeing reality and of understanding man, though enlarged, remained essentially the same.

The truth was quite different. There was, first of all, a radical change in the manner in which man was seen. Hence there was also a radical change in the manner in which man's relations with other beings were seen. As a result of this change, the whole rich

----
[2] Kepler, *Harmonice mundi*, IV, 6–7; *Gesammelte Werke*, Munich, 1930, vol. VI, pp. 257, 266ff., 285.

array of motifs which had been suppressed, condemned, and exorcised as so many empty and diabolical obsessions, started to come to the fore to reveal
their fruitful aspects, becoming purified in the process without actually losing their original meaning.
For this reason one finds during the Renaissance a
great many discussions about the possibility of dis-
tinguishing true magic from false magic, true astrology from false astrology, true alchemy from false
alchemy. For people sensed that here was a new way
which might allow man to gain a full mastery over
nature. The attempt to seize precisely those methods
which medieval theology had rejected shows once
again how fundamental the break with the middle
ages had really been.

It is worth dwelling on this point at some length.
During the fifteenth century the new image of man
had reached full self-consciousness and assumed its
characteristic dimensions under the aegis of Hermes
Trismegistos. It came to be developed along the lines
fixed once and for all in the Hermetic books. In spite
of the fact that there was a clear distinction between
the *Poimander*, the *Asclepius*, and the theological
writings on one side, and the innumerable magico-
alchemical treatises on the other, one ought never to
forget that there was a very subtle and profound subterranean link that connected the former to the occult, astrological, and alchemical traditions of the
latter.[3] The point of agreement between the two lay
precisely in the idea that the universe was alive, that
it was full of hidden correspondences, of occult
sympathies, and that it was completely pervaded by
spirits, all of them refracting signs pregnant with
hidden meanings. In this universe every thing, every
being, every force was like a voice not yet fully understood, like a word suspended in mid-air. It was a universe in which every word had innumerable echoes

---

[3] This has been clearly emphasised by Festugière.

and resonances, in which the stars were sending messages and listening to us and to each other, were looking at us and looking at each other. This universe was an immensely multiple and varied form of speech, now soft and now loud, now in secret messages, now in disclosed sentences. In the middle there was man, a miraculous being, subject to change, a being capable of uttering all words, transforming all things, and drawing all characters, a being capable of responding to every call and calling every god.[4]

The beautiful opening lines of the *Asclepius* had already proved seductive to the Fathers of the Church, who had tried in vain to exorcise them. In our period these lines began to resound with their original solemn strength: "Man is a great miracle, worthy of honour and veneration." In this work, man is seen as immortal, suspended between heaven and earth; unique among all beings of the lower world he is forever hurling himself beyond himself, like a vivified flame. He dominates the world through his work, he defies the elements, knows the demons, mixes with spirits. He transforms everything and fashions divine images. A poet was to say that the immortal gods descend from the heavens in order to look with envy upon the graven images which the artist has made of them. Among so many stable things, man is quite unstable himself, like the fire which burns and consumes, destroys and refashions. He has no one face because he has a thousand different faces, and he has no one form because he dissolves all forms and is reborn in every one of them. He owns them all and makes them his own. For this reason, the *Asclepius* tells us, the chorus of the Muses has descended to mankind, for here, in this musical convergence of the

---

[4] I am using the technical terms of astrology. Ptolomaeus, *Tetrab.*, I, 15–16; Firm. Mat., VIII, 2: *videntium et audientium stellarum theorica. . . .*

world, one finds the realm of that true poetry which alone is true creation.

Augustine, in *The City of God* recalls the sad Hermetic prophecy which went as follows: "Egypt, Egypt, your gods will be remembered only in legends. Future generations will find it hard to believe in their existence and only their names will remain carved on stones. Once men are gone, the weeping gods will return to their heavenly abodes." But here, at the moment that ancient wisdom was reborn, the Egyptian prophet, who appears so majestically in the mosaic of the Cathedral of Siena, was a visible testimony of the return of that ancient wisdom. Long before the divine Marsilio Ficino translated them into Latin and long before his friend Tommaso Benci translated them from Latin into the Tuscan vernacular, indeed ever since the earliest beginnings of Humanism, the words of Hermes Trismegistos had come to dominate the minds of all those who were singing the praises of man. Salutati paid his respects to him. The judicious Giannozzo Manetti knew him through Lactantius. And by the middle of the fifteenth century, Ficino was demanding that everyone follow him. The translation of the *Poimander* spread not only through Italy but through the whole of Europe. It redeemed the subterranean and mysterious Hermetic doctrines and turned them into a new cult. Poets sang of it in elaborate Latin verses, Lorenzo the Magnificent praised it in vernacular verses and Gelli, the shoemaker philosopher, expounded it in lively dialogues in Florence. During the last decades of the fifteenth century an enthusiastic disciple preached it in the streets of the capital of Christendom, accompanying it with strange rites and a priestly ceremonial, distributing printed prayers and propaganda leaflets. Sculpted in Cathedrals, worshipped in Rome, the object of poetry in Florence, discussed in the Academies, the voice of Hermes, Three Times Great, was heard even from the venerable chairs in universities: the professors in response to a general need and a general taste discussed him in their courses. Political as well as religious orators alluded to him, using him rather than Aristotle or the Fathers of the Church for suitable quotations with which to adorn their speeches.[5]

The picture of man presented by the "Prince of Concord" in his oration is shot through with Hermetic ideas: the characteristic of man is not so much that he is the centre of the universe as that he can liberate himself from the realm of forms and is the lord of his own nature precisely because he has no fixed nature of his own. Since man has no particular nature and is therefore the point at which liberty is total, the world of forms is subject to man. He is thus able to reach beyond it in the sense that he can degenerate into demonism as well as ascend towards the deity and the super-intellectual. The miraculous character of man consists in the singular fact that he is suspended in the centre of the determinate reasons for things. Because of this, the whole of nature, all other beings, and all finite reasons depend somehow on his decision. Man is capable of sweeping away everything by dissolution. Similarly he can redeem everything by a liberating transfiguration. All things are fixed forever in their condition: stones, animals, plants, and the stars in their courses. By contrast, man is nothing, but capable of becoming everything. He is extended towards the future. His humanity consists not in a given nature, but in the fact that he can make himself, that he can choose. It allows him to free himself

---

[5] All this is well known. Cp. C. Bonardi, "Le orazioni di Lorenzo dei Medici e l'inno finale della 'Circe' di G. B. Belli," *Giornale storico della Letteratura italiana*, XXXIII, 1899. P. O. Kristeller, "Marsilio Ficino e Ludovico Lazzarelli," *Annali Scuola Normale Superiore Pisa*, 1938. Cornelius Agrippa read the *Poimander* in 1515 in Pavia. See *Opera*, Lugduni, 1600, Vol. II, p. 401.

from the confines of reality. Since he has no face, he consists of his work. That work is what he chooses to do with things and it consists of the imprint he leaves on the world, i.e. the way he shapes and reshapes the world. Every time a discussion of magic turned upon the idea that the universe falls or rises through the will of man, i.e. of Adam, and that it is governed either by a demon or by God, this idea was charged with a very precise and revolutionary meaning. The old medieval image of an order of which man was a part was broken. Man now stood between the realm in which there was no form, the realm of the devil, and the absolute realm without bounds, which was God. Man can avail himself of ordered forms to sublimate things in God or to hurl them into the darkness of abnormality, the monstrous, and the chaotic. The controversy between true, natural magic and ceremonial magic amounted to this. True magic was defended because it was work which made use of the given forms in order to construct an ascending chain of Being. Ceremonial magic, on the other hand, was attacked because it was work which led into the abyss of sin and chaos. In both cases, however, the ambiguous reality of man consisted in the fact that he was a possibility, an opening through which one could rejoice in the inexhaustible richness of Being. He was not a being, defined once and for all, immobile and secure, but was always precariously balanced upon the margin of an absolute risk.

The distance between the middle ages and the new age is the distance between a closed universe, an unchanging, static world which has no history and an infinite universe which is open to all possibilities. In the system of the medieval universe, magic was no more than a demonic temptation, bent upon making a crack in a peaceful and perfect world. As such, magic was opposed, persecuted, and burnt. It was something that could not be included among the sciences worthy of man. It was no more than a descent into chaos, a yielding to devilish seduction. Men who practised it were seduced by the monstrous. There could never be any agreement between medieval philosophy and magic; for medieval philosophy was a theology of order, articulated temporarily as Aristotelianism. That theology preferred looking upon man as nothing but a mere member of the human species to facing the scandal that would have resulted if it had considered man freed from the bonds of the order of nature. It could never have entertained the notion that man might use nature as an instrument, understand it and, through understanding it, proclaim it to be purely provisional. Theology was bound to prefer the rationality that resulted from security and from a lack of historical consciousness. It could not reconcile itself to the idea that man was free to gamble with what was alleged to be the structure of the universe.

In conformity with these theological views, both magic and astrology were, in the middle ages, the realm of the demoniacal which subsisted below the limits of reason. Both magic and astrology were taken to operate outside the sphere of reason. They operated among the elements in a region in which contingency allowed a certain efficacy to human effort. Both were the sciences of experimentation. But on the level on which beings existed in an orderly scale, on the level of reason, there was no room for contingency and the future was completely determined by the past. On that level the notion of experience was nonsensical, for the rigorous chain of syllogistic reasoning completely predetermined the totality of existent beings. For this reason, any contingency which might be revealed by an experiment could only be located in the region below the level of rational intelligence. Since the whole of the Lord's creation was a neat and well-ordered house, medieval theologians considered the proper seat of contingent experience to be in the realm of evil—i.e. in the abyss which existed before the beginning of the world or in the hell which is the abode of all those who have become estranged from the world. Such a primacy of logic, and of the idea that mathematics occupied a privileged position as an *a priori* condition of the universe, is a great danger to the conception of man and of history and, in the end, even to the idea of God; at least to the idea of the God in Heaven, the God Who is a person and of the God Who is Man, the God of Abraham, Isaac, and Jacob. But in the middle ages the universe, organised in eternal spheres of rotation, was opposed by the dominion of demons in which the magician practised his arts. And thus the magician was a man who had been chased from rational reality and had found refuge among ever-changing apparitions. He was a man who evoked shadows, gazed into regions of monstrous deities, and sensed that behind man there were turgid and obscure forces. The era in which magicians and astrology were condemned was the era in which magic was considered a subhuman science, a necromancy, and in which judicial astrology was associated with ceremonial magic. In that era the ancient powers of darkness that populated the heavens with monstrous apparitions were induced by prayers and rites to work upon the parallel forces of darkness that surged up from the depth of chaos. There is, of course, a certain similarity between some astrological doctrines and the theory of the unconscious: both find expression in mythology and bear witness to a world wilfully and forcefully suppressed. Whereas theology rationally relegated to an unreal sphere of evil all those impulses that batter against the borders of the realm of order, magic cultivated them, examined them, experimented with them, and made use of them. Faced by living forms solidly cast in the hierarchy of unchanging species, it sought strange marriages and dreamt of monstrous achievements and diabolical creations.[6] Beneath the perfect and uniform circles of purely crystalline heavenly spheres, the astrologer caught glimpses of malign radiations, of the sun burning the powers of the planets, of lethal emanations left behind by the stars on their courses, of stars which laugh in one place and cry in another, of beasts trembling under their fateful stare. He saw furious battles raging among the monsters of the zodiac and deities who emerged in the weirdest of garbs, black Ethiopians with eyes of fire and white virgins carrying bundles of corn.[7]

Ristoro d'Arezzo, in the beginning of his *Composizione del mondo*, wrote that this our abode is like a well-ordered house or, rather, like a solemn temple in which the sky with its clusters of stars is like a stained glass of holy images, carrying messages from a God rising amidst choirs of angels. The astrologer saw more than those windows. He saw horrible forces hidden beyond the small region in which reason holds sway. He saw man suspended over an abyss and man with an abyss inside him. He mused about dreams and visions, on the strange resistance of the body, on brutal impulses, on the passions, on diseases, on pain and death. He saw strange connections between monsters and miracles, between folly and saintliness, between prophetic

---

[6] Some of these allusions are to the pseudoplatonic *Liber Vaccae* and to the famous *Picatrix* which I have read in the Florentine ms., *Naz.*, II, III, 214, and *Magl.*, XX, 20.

[7] For these images see Cornelius Agrippa, *de occ. philos.* II, 37. Giordano Bruni, *De umbris idearum*, Naples, ed. by Imbriani and Tallarigo, 1866, pp. 135–57, is dependent on Agrippa. One of the classical sources is the *Introductorium* by Albumasar. It was reproduced by Boll, *Sphaera*, pp. 490ff., in the original Arabic version by Dyroff, together with a German translation. Ibn Ezra, the source for Pietro d'Abano, derives from Albumasar. There is a German version of these texts in Gundel, *Dekane und Dekansternbilder*, Glueckstadt and Hamburg, 1936.

visions and hallucinations. All in all, he was obsessed by evil, by the evil which is incomprehensible in a universe made by God. He was equally obsessed by life, which was also incomprehensible because it could not be assigned a place in the eternal and unchanging rhythm of reason. In this way, the whole of living nature kept sliding into the opaque realm of the occult. And so did the miracles, the sacred symbols, the Cross, and the Virgin. What did Christ, who was born of a virgin and died on a cross, or God the Father Who is in Heaven, Who loves and is loved, Who suffers and Who made so ephemeral a being as man, have to do with the geometrical rationality of the heavenly spheres, with the immobile light of the pure act, wholly complete in itself throughout eternity? And while the astrologer watched Trivia laugh with joy among the eternal Nymphs, the magician sought to listen to the forces which kept agitating the most intimate parts of all beings and to the spirits which resolve in the midst of all things. Both magician and astrologer saw human passions joined to the profound movement of all being. They intended to make use of the complex energies which lie below the plain surface of thought.

In criticising astrology it has often been repeated that astrology conceived the origin of the world in such a way that it amounted to placing existence in chains and lowered the conception of man because it placed him among mere objects. The truth was quite different. The heavens of the astrologers did not behave like the mechanical heavens of the post-Galilean age. After Galileo, astrology tended if anything towards a complete humanisation of the world, rather than towards a naturalisation of man. In the age before Galileo the heavenly spheres, populated by living spirits, were not so much a nature which oppressed man as an enlargement of man in the direction of endless change, in eternal interchange with the immortal beings who animated the stars and the houses of the sky. In this conception, human destiny was not determined once and for all, but its course was at the mercy of the multitude of deities who ruled the several temples. These lords of time were like the divine princes who issued their orders to the forces that regulate the elements. We find a mythology in place of celestial mechanics, to the extent that we find orders and prayers, assaults and defences, liturgy and rhetoric in place of mathematical calculations. The sage dominates the stars—as a solemn maxim, frequently quoted in manuals of astrology, put it. He rules the stars because he can turn the line which descends from the stars to man upside down, that is, into a line which ascends from man to the stars. The wise man not only benefits from the margin of possibility which appears wherever forces meet and are balanced, but also is able to influence, through conscious strategy, divine astral powers.

Instead of concentrating on discussions of the origins of the universe, we ought to take a look at one of the many treatments of election and interrogation. Man is uncertain as to what he ought to do, when he wants to travel or marry, when he wants to found a city or a kingdom. Therefore he goes to an astrologer or a necromancer. His destiny has been determined by the hour of his conception or birth as read in the quadrant of the sky. But it is also possible, and one ought to keep this in mind, that what has been determined is his bodily structure, his temperament, the whole substratum of his mental life. According to the hierarchical conception, his mental life is not governed but merely influenced by his physical, organic, and natural make-up. He now wants to know, given his general condition, whether, in the limits imposed on him by nature, his plan is likely to succeed.

How does the astrologer go about it? He knows that astral influences work upon deep forces and he also knows that the line of orientation which is present in all parts of the universe leaves a subterranean trace in himself as well as in the man who consults him. He knows that the directive cosmic forces work in everything and upon everything and that all one needs is to consult the voice of the stars. But in order to hear that voice, one has to silence one's own voice. The conceptual limit has to leave room for elemental motion. In order to achieve this, he seeks to suspend the lucid conscious control of the man who consults him. He makes him trace out in the sand certain points of departure so that, when the situation has been mapped out, he can suggest to him, through appropriate means, how the stars can be controlled. The wise man, like a God of the earth, once he has understood the natural order, can, by obeying it, turn it upside down.

Historians have often expressed surprise that a pious Franciscan like Roger Bacon or a Cardinal of the Holy Roman Church like Peter d'Ailly or a fundamentally orthodox Dominican like Thomas Campanella should have entertained the idea that one could work out a horoscope for religions. According to this idea the changes in religious cults and, e.g. the coming of the prophets, are determined by the grand conjunctions of the planets. It amounts to the belief that God has arranged the forces of nature in such a way as to carry the message of the birth of His Son—a birth which was in fact announced by the star that appeared to the Three Wise Men. For the astrologer as well as for the magician, nature is all of a piece and embraces man, who can scrutinise her soul and mould her through prayers as well as through incantations and thus turn her plasticity to his own advantage.

Magic medicine possesses a revelatory power. The physician makes use of images and prayers in order to compel deep forces and hidden powers and to excite the spirits of the sick man, to change and heal diseased organs. Avicenna was a great physician and his books dominated the faculties of medicine right down to the end of the seventeenth century. He insisted that the soul is omnipotent and that words, signs, and symbols are capable of assisting a man to regain his health. Similarly Antonio Benivieni, who was a fervent admirer of Savonarola as well as a distinguished physician and scientist, reported that Friar Domenico da Pescia had been able to heal, among others, the learned Robert Salviati by praying intensively with the sick man and by making the sign of the cross over the organ which was sick. Marsilio Ficino, a physician among other things, had no hesitation in attributing the power of the sign of the cross to the importance assigned to it by astrologers and magicians outside the realm of Christianity. Benivieni, Ficino, and Pomponazzi, invoking Avicenna and Roger Bacon, interpreted the healing power of the cross as a nervous tension or a tension of spirits. They believed that this tension was brought about by suitable means and was capable of modifying bodily conditions, conditions which were in fact subject to spirits.[8]

The intellectual scaffolding of medieval theological thought had results which are comparable to the results of the extreme rationalism of modern times. Reality is broken up because firm logical concepts are opposed to the never-ending plasticity of life. The soul is pitted against the body; reason against the passions; spirit against nature; a rigorous uniformity of laws against the absurdity of miracles; cool knowledge against the heat of action. The magico-astrological standpoints were based on the notion that reality consists of a basic unity which causes the sparkling of the most distant star to have repercussions even in

---

[8] Ficino, De vita, III, 18. A. Benivieni, De abditis, is well known. But I am also making use of a medico-magical treatise on Avicenna by the Imola physician A. Cattani, published in Florence at the beginning of the sixteenth century.

the most hidden corner of the world; and conversely, on the notion that every single movement of the soul found an echo in the most infinite of vibrations. In the universe there were no fissures: there were only vast numbers of correspondences in the living flow of the totality of life.

In the first years of the fourteenth century, the astrologer and physician Pietro d'Abano had been taught by the observations of people's faces that every physiognomy mirrors the intimacy of the heart. He knew that in everything which is visible there is hidden a deeper meaning. He wrote that the stars, provided we carry out the necessary gestures, can be placated and will move to help us and favour us. When Isabella d'Este in 1509 mourned the imprisonment of her husband, she consulted the distinguished astrologer Pellegrino de' Prisciani. He reminded her of the words in the *Conciliatore* to the effect that the kings of Greece when they sought a special favour from God had waited for opportune heavenly constellations to occur and had then made their prayer. He advised her that such a powerful and blessed constellation was about to occur on the following Saturday, that it had been expected by astrologers and wise men for many years. He suggested that she spend that day in the most ardent concentration of prayer, that at the specified hour she direct her eyes to heaven, kneel down and fold her hands, that she confess from the depths of her heart, saying the *confiteor*, and that she then ask of God in the most suitable words that might occur to her whether he would not by grace condescend to restore her beloved husband to her free and healthy and safe. If she would repeat her request three times God would grant the favour after a short time.

As one can see, astrological practice was very far from assuming that events were dominated by an iron fate, part of a rigorous mechanism. There were spells, incantations, and talismans, for everything was alive and animated and man was always able, through the living ministers of God, the stars, to invoke God. In one of the most famous manuals of magic of the middle ages we find the following prayer to the sun, supposed to be recited before anybody could obtain the king's favour: "Oh you, who are the root of heaven, above all stars, above all planets, holy and honoured . . . you who are the light of the world, I invoke you by all your names . . . I implore you in the name of Him Who has given you light and life."

It was no accident that of all people it was a Franciscan, Roger Bacon, who when he opened his eyes and mind to the fact that all life is movement, worked out the most fervent defence of astrology and magic. In his view all relations were ultimately personal relations rather than numbers and measures and causes. Sun and moon were brother and sister; water was a sister and the wolf a brother and all other created beings were brothers and sisters and God was their father. This personal conception took the place of a network of logical essences. It appeared as an ever-new play of existences and was always open to all possibilities and capable of yielding to persuasion. This doctrine remained popular throughout the Renaissance and it commanded respect right down to the dawn of Newtonian physics. Campanella presented it in a poetical guise when he taught that everything was alive, animated, mobile, and plastic. The implication of this doctrine was that the universe is infinite, truly absolute, that there are no barriers, and that it is without internal or external limits. This also was the meaning of Giordano Bruno when he prided himself on having abolished all boundaries of the world. The demolition of these boundaries and the defeat of all monsters meant that he did not see the roots of life outside the rigid limits of an iron set of concepts, but that he believed in the unity of the one fundamental vital impetus which is both form and matter, a free possibility without end, a flow of energy which shapes its own order and at the same time transcends it. He taught that there is an act which constitutes being and that no static being can ever extinguish the life of that act. He also rejected the contemplation of inert, definite essences and laboured instead at the convergence of knowledge and action and at a science which is at the service of a magical transformation of the universe. ". . . the earth and her oceans are fertile and the blaze of the sun is eternal . . . for the infinite always gives birth to a new lot of matter." If Bruno says "matter," we must have no illusions about his meaning. In the infinite in which we are living and which is living within us "there is no matter, because it cannot take shape and has never taken shape; it is not definable and has never been defined. It has no form because it gives no form . . . but its only form consists in its not having form; and it is matter only insofar as it is not material; and it is soul insofar as it is not a soul: for it is the All, one, infinite, living, absolute."

Ever since the nineteenth century, and perhaps even ever since the age of Enlightenment and Rationalism, historians have looked upon the Renaissance as a preparation for the divorce between pure reason, science, and Cartesianism, and the dark, vital, and obscure forces, the spirits of the heavens and of things. Burckhardt used to say that the latter were the relics of misty, medieval superstitions. The truth is however that during the Renaissance, people were fighting *against* a divorce of this kind in order to bring about a new convergence between rational understanding and occult forces. At the time of the Renaissance the security of a historical cosmic order was destroyed. The idea that there existed fixed structures and a conceptual hierarchy which rejected everything that was not part of the universal form was dissolved. The idea of man as a purely contemplative subject was abandoned and so was the idea that man was a being who has to suppress his flesh and his passions and make himself blind to every seduction life has to offer. For people ceased to believe that man ought to make his own reason impersonal so that it could be joined to universal reason. Instead of a human skeleton which moved in a world consisting of other geometrical skeletons, there emerged the Hermetic idea that will, work, and action produce and dissolve forms, that there is universal creativity moving freely with an aim towards the future which is infinite and infinitely open and in which everything is possible. According to this ideal the universe as a set of inexhaustible possibilities corresponded to the man who is engaged in creative work. In this universe there was no force which could not be bent by wise precautions and no destiny which could not be controlled and no star which did not understand human language, no energy which could not be made use of. In the infinite and living unity all limitations were abolished forever.

Bruno taught us in a famous passage that the wise man is the man who researches not by grasping totality through dead concepts but by capturing the infinitely living unity of the universe, by making himself one with the creative power which is none other than the Creator Himself. Thus Actaeon pursued Diana; but when he beheld her in the nude, the dogs devoured him: "The dogs are the thoughts of divine things and they devoured Actaeon and in devouring him, loosened the bonds which held . . . his perturbed senses in captivity. Hence he could no longer behold his Diana through windows, but with the walls broken down, he became all eye, open to the whole of the horizon. And seeing that everything is One he was no longer aware of distinctions and numbers . . . he could now behold Amphitrite, the source of all numbers, of all species, of all reasons, for it is the Monad, the true essence of every thing."

The infinite power of man is gathered in the unity

of the act. Here we have the wise man who dominates the stars, the magician who can shape the elements. Here we have the unity of thought and being and here we have the whole of reality open in front of us. This and nothing else was intended by the defence of magic. And it was for this reason that the Renaissance added the art of magic to the reasons why man ought to be praised.

of the arts. Long we have, because man who doubt-
inner once saw the endeavour who can shape the
tongue. Here we have the unity of thought, no
being made more alive; the whole of being a certain
through of ... ... and manner who was beyond by
... definite of magic. And because ... able found the
... Renaissance added the art of magic to the reason
... who may must to be perfect.

INDEX